D0864391

Crisis? What crisis? Orderly workouts for sovereign debtors

Barry Eichengreen
Richard Portes

Francesca Cornelli
Leonardo Felli
Julian Franks
Christopher Greenwood
Hugh Mercer
Giovanni Vitale

SUFFOLK UNIVERSITY
MILDRED F. SAWYER LIBRARY
8 ASHBURTON PLACE
BOSTON, MA 02108

DISCARDED BY
SUFFOLK UNIVERSITY
SAWYER LIBRARY

Centre for Economic Policy Research

The Centre for Economic Policy Research is a network of 300 Research Fellows, based primarily in European universities. The Centre coordinates its Fellows' research activities and communicates their results to the public and private sectors. CEPR is an entrepreneur, developing research initiatives with the producers, consumers and sponsors of research. Established in 1983, CEPR is a European economics research organization with uniquely wide-ranging scope and activities.

CEPR is a registered educational charity. Institutional (core) finance for the Centre is provided by major grants from the Economic and Social Research Council, under which an ESRC Resource Centre operates within CEPR; the Esmée Fairbairn Charitable Trust; the Bank of England; 17 other central banks and 40 companies. None of these organizations gives prior review to the Centre's publications, nor do they necessarily endorse the views expressed therein.

The Centre is pluralist and non-partisan, bringing economic research to bear on the analysis of medium- and long-run policy questions. CEPR research may include views on policy, but the Executive Committee of the Centre does not give prior review to its publications, and the Centre takes no institutional policy positions. The opinions expressed in this report are those of the authors and not those of the Centre for Economic Policy Research.

Executive Committee
Chairman   Anthony Loehnis
Vice-Chairman   Guillermo de la Dehesa

Jan Bielecki   Philippe Lagayette
Honor Chapman   Peter Middleton
Quentin Davies   David Miliband
Sheila Drew Smith   Mario Sarcinelli
Otmar Issing   Catherine Sweet
Mervyn King

Officers
Director   Richard Portes
Deputy Director   Stephen Yeo

1 September 1995

Published by Centre for Economic Policy Research
25–28 Old Burlington Street, London W1X 1LB

© Centre for Economic Policy Research

British Library Cataloguing in Publication Data
A Catalogue record for this book is available from the British Library

ISBN: 1 898128 23 5

HJ
8083
.C74
1995

Contents

List of Contributors

Francesca Cornelli *London Business School and CEPR*
Barry Eichengreen *University of California, Berkeley, and CEPR*
Leonardo Felli *London School of Economics*
Julian Franks *London Business School and CEPR*
Christopher Greenwood *Magdalene College, Cambridge,
and Essex Court Chambers*
Hugh Mercer *Essex Court Chambers*
Richard Portes *London Business School and CEPR*
Giovanni Vitale *Birkbeck College, London*

Foreword

Thirteen years ago, at the IMF/World Bank Annual Meetings in Washington in 1982, the international financial and banking community was faced with what became known as the international debt crisis. The handling of that crisis was to preoccupy many members of this community in both the public and private sectors for the best part of a decade. It can be convincingly argued that the outcome was a considerable success: the international banking system did not melt down, and the majority of the indebted countries emerged from an undoubtedly painful experience with much improved economic policies and expectations.

Yet it was less than a year ago that the first victim of the crisis and perhaps the most successful exemplar of the rehabilitation process – Mexico – was once again at the centre of a national debt crisis which threatened the same domino reaction that had unfolded in the 1980s. In spite of the earlier experiences, few lessons appeared to have been learned, and the handling of the recent crisis exhibited the same *ad-hocery* and provoked as much controversy as the handling of the earlier one.

It has been said that those who cannot remember the past are condemned to repeat it. Much effort has been made to draw lessons from earlier debt crises, but no two crises are precisely the same. Financial instruments, institutions and structures change over very short periods, as does the national and international climate within which debt workouts take place. CEPR is pleased therefore to have been commissioned earlier this summer by HM Treasury, the Bank of England and the Foreign and Commonwealth Office to carry out a research project to examine whether there are lessons to be learned from the debt-restructuring experience of the 1980s and earlier periods, which could point the way towards a more orderly approach to the resolution of future sovereign debt crises and command a measure of international agreement.

The project was directed by Barry Eichengreen and Richard Portes, well known as historians and analysts of earlier sovereign debt issues, and they were supported by contributions from Francesca Cornelli, Leonardo Felli, Julian Franks, Christopher Greenwood and Hugh Mercer, as well as research assistance from Giovanni Vitale.

The outcome is this report, which has been produced within a period of less than three months. We are very grateful to CEPR's Publications Assistant, James MacGregor, who enabled such a tight time constraint to be met.

One clear lesson of the 1980s is that all-embracing blueprints for debt relief will not command consensus and thus will not succeed. Based on a knowledge of history, an analysis of the motivations of the participants and sensibility to the difficulties of reaching international consensus, this timely report points more modestly to a pragmatic agenda of reform, which could improve the atmosphere and framework within which future sovereign debt restructurings can be worked out.

Anthony Loehnis
21 September 1995

The authors gratefully acknowledge the funding and support they have received from HM Treasury, the Bank of England and the Foreign and Commonwealth Office, who sponsored this research as a contribution to the current international debate on options for more orderly workout procedures. The study by Barry Eichengreen and Richard Portes also reflects comments from participants drawn from the public and private sectors at a seminar hosted by the Bank of England on 19 September 1995.

The conclusions are the sole responsibility of the authors and do not represent the official policy of Her Majesty's Government or the Bank of England.

Executive summary

The Mexican crisis of 1994–5 has stimulated much discussion of new institutions and procedures for managing financial crises in heavily indebted countries. While these proposals come under various names – orderly workouts, bankruptcy procedures, binding arbitration and debt adjustment facilities – the underlying motivation is the same. They respond to the view that it is possible to improve upon existing conventions and arrangements for dealing with such crises. As it is, there are few alternatives to either 'throwing money at the problem' with a bailout from official funds or keeping hands off in a way that runs the risk of chaos and contagion. Delineating a third option is the goal of this report.

We see five concerns about the way financial markets, governments and multilateral institutions respond to 'Mexico-style' crises. First, the market's violent reaction to financial difficulties (in the form of a self-fulfilling 'run') forces governments to adopt drastic monetary and fiscal austerity packages that threaten to destabilize output, employment and economic growth. Over-reaction by investors, who face a problem of collective action, is a market failure from which improved institutions and procedures could offer greater insulation.

Second, debts are restructured, if at all, only after a protracted period of discussion and negotiation. This reflects the prevalence of asymmetric information and negotiating costs. Improved institutions and procedures would disseminate information and facilitate negotiations. They would encourage a quicker resolution to crises and reduce the need for public funds where debt restructuring was at issue.

Third, the markets find it difficult to coordinate the provision of new money where this is needed by countries undergoing liquidity crises. Improved institutions and procedures could help to overcome this problem of coordination failure, facilitating the injection of new funds where an orderly restructuring of existing debts is not enough.

Fourth, appropriate management roles for national governments and multilateral institutions have not been defined. The *ad hoc* response of the IMF and the US government to the Mexican crisis is unlikely to be repeated. G–7 leaders agreed at the June 1995 Halifax Summit to double the General Arrangements to Borrow and to establish a new mechanism for emergency financing to deal with Mexico-like problems, but the procedures themselves are as yet unclear.

Fifth and finally, while everyone agrees on the desirability of preventing crises in the first place, there is no consensus on how this might be done.

Proposals have appeared that address these concerns. Recommendations include promoting changes in the provisions of loan contracts and bond covenants; government support for the creation of bondholders' steering committees; expanding the signalling and mediation roles of the IMF; creating a venue for negotiations involving bondholders' representatives, the government of the indebted country and the IMF; closing the courts of creditor countries to dissident creditors by statute or treaty or by invoking Article VIII(2)(b) of the IMF Articles of Agreement; and establishing a bankruptcy procedure for sovereign debtors analogous to Chapter 11 of the US bankruptcy code.

We find problems with each of these proposals. The creation of bondholders' committees would not halt the creditors' rush for the exits, and although securitized debt is more important now than in the 1980s, it is not the only source of problems. Countries that have been reluctant to suspend debt service payments unilaterally for fear of damaging their reputations would have no incentive to behave differently. Settlements would still take time, and the injection of new money would remain difficult. Measures to strengthen collateralization will be difficult to enforce. Assigning responsibility for debts to quasi-public enterprises rather than the central government is no guarantee against a bailout. Self-imposed debt limits place the fiscal authorities in a macroeconomic straitjacket and are unlikely to be credible. Closing the courts to creditors by statute or treaty would prevent a small band of dissident creditors from using legal means to hold up a restructuring but would not address the other problems with current procedures. Using IMF Article VIII(2)(b) to enforce a payments standstill encounters legal difficulties.

An international court or tribunal with powers analogous to those enjoyed by bankruptcy courts in the United States is a non-starter, given the very great legal obstacles to implementation. If such obstacles were to be surmounted, the desirability of such a procedure remains unclear. Even operating under a treaty, such an international court would be unlikely to possess the powers of a national court to enforce seizure of collateral, given sovereign immunity. It would not be able to replace the government of a country the way bankruptcy courts replace the management of firms. The danger of moral hazard would be great.

Nevertheless, each of these proposals has desirable features. We therefore offer an agenda for reform which combines elements of the alternative approaches. A quick initial reaction to a gathering crisis is essential, and our first recommendation is that the IMF should more actively transmit signals about the advisability of temporary unilateral payments standstills. Governments can impose the equivalent of a standstill by suspending debt service payments. But they hesitate to do so for fear that they will jeopardize their future credit market access. Encouraging the IMF to advise the debtor and issue opinions on the justifiability of a stay of payments would give the Fund an important signalling function; a government which received approval for its standstill would suffer relatively little damage to its reputation, while the possibility that the Fund would not approve would discourage governments from utilizing the option strategically. Naturally, the IMF should limit its advice to the debtor government before the fact and share its opinion with the markets only *ex post*. A definitive reinterpretation of Article VIII(2)(b) would support the IMF in this role even if it did not have legal effect in national courts.

Creating a Bondholders Council would eliminate uncertainty about the locus of authority in negotiations. It would be responsible for restructuring bonded debts, while the London and Paris Clubs would retain their responsibility for bank loans and official credits. Discussions between the debtor and the Paris Club, the London Club and the Bondholders Council would rely on a specially constituted conciliation and mediation service designed to minimize the danger of an extended deadlock.

Changes in bond covenants to permit a majority of creditors to alter the terms of payment would prevent dissident investors from holding up the settlement. To make this palatable to potential lenders, dissident creditors would have recourse to an arbitral tribunal. To prevent a negotiated agreement or the findings of the arbitral tribunal from being disputed in court, loan agreements would specify that objections by minority creditors be subject to the tribunal's arbitration.

Strengthened IMF monitoring and conditionality would reduce the likelihood that financial problems will recur. The knowledge that any new money injected in conjunction with the debt restructuring, and even Fund sanction for a country's unilateral standstill, would be predicated on the government's first agreeing to fulfil stringent IMF conditions, would work to minimize the likelihood of such difficulties arising in the first place. Frequent monitoring by the IMF of economic conditions in debtor countries and timely dissemination of information by the Fund would strengthen market discipline. Increased resources available to the Fund would allow, where appropriate, injection of new money on the requisite scale.

It would be possible to adopt some of these recommendations without also embracing others. But there are important complementarities among the reforms we propose. They would do most to enhance the efficiency of the debt restructuring process if implemented as a package.

As the experience of economies in transition has reminded us, markets are *social institutions*: they function properly only within a well-defined legal and institutional framework. Some of these institutions can develop spontaneously, in a decentralized fashion; others must be created by concerted action. Thus helping to construct the framework is not inappropriate official intervention in the market place, but rather helping the market to work (what in post-war German economic policy analysis is called *Ordnungspolitik*). We hope that the proposals here may contribute to that effort.

Crisis? What crisis?
Orderly workouts for sovereign debtors

Barry Eichengreen
University of California, Berkeley, and CEPR

Richard Portes
London Business School and CEPR

1   Introduction

The Mexican crisis of 1994–5 has stimulated much discussion of new institutions and procedures for managing financial crises in heavily indebted countries. While these proposals come under various names – orderly workouts, bankruptcy procedures, binding arbitration and debt adjustment facilities – the underlying motivation is the same. They respond to the view that it is possible to improve upon existing conventions and arrangements for dealing with crises like that experienced by Mexico in the winter of 1994–5. As it is, there appear to be few alternatives to either 'throwing money at the problem' with a bailout from official funds or keeping hands off in a way that runs the risk of chaos and contagion. Delineating a third option is the goal of this report.

This approach should have the following characteristics. It would allow quick action to halt the creditors' rush for the exits, preventing the panic from destabilizing the country's banking system and severely dislocating its economy. It would facilitate the quick conclusion of debt restructuring negotiations between bondholders, banks, official creditors and the indebted government. Where an injection of funds was deemed essential to prevent the crisis from spilling over into the banking system or spreading contiguously to other markets, the pump could be primed by the limited provision of funds by the IMF. This would be conditional on the government's implementation of policy reforms which would encourage the market to supplement the official funds and limit the need for the latter. Crisis management measures would be administered in an incentive-compatible way that encouraged governments to release information on economic conditions in a timely fashion and that discouraged them from pursuing policies that might provoke a crisis in the first place.

Interpretations of the Mexican episode vary, and similar situations would play themselves out differently in other times and places. Nonetheless, this experience pointed out five reasons why current procedures fail to deliver these results.

Market over-reaction. The market's violent reaction to financial difficulties forces governments to adopt drastic monetary and fiscal austerity packages that threaten to destabilize output, employment and economic growth. Investors face a collective action problem: each individual investor has an incentive to rush for the exits, even if the creditors are better off as a group if they all continue to hold the country's debt. In Mexico the rush for the exits forced the government to raise interest rates to triple-digit levels and the economy was plunged into a serious recession, with real GDP in the second quarter of 1995 down by 10% from a year earlier. Over-reaction by investors, who face a problem of collective action, is a market failure from which improved institutions and procedures could offer greater insulation.[1]

Protracted negotiations. Debts are restructured, if at all, only after a protracted period of discussion and negotiation. Historically, settlement of defaulted bonded sovereign debt has often taken years to complete. In Mexico orderly restructuring proved impossible within the narrow window of time that market pressures left open.[2] This reflects the prevalence of asymmetric information and negotiating costs. Improved institutions and procedures would disseminate information and facilitate negotiations. They would encourage a quick resolution to crises and reduce the need for public funds where debt restructuring was at issue.

Inability to inject new money. Private markets find it difficult to coordinate the provision of new money where this is needed by countries undergoing liquidity crises that threaten, *inter alia*, the stability of their banking systems. This is particularly problematic in the case of bond finance, when it is necessary to coordinate the actions of a large number of individual investors and limit free-rider behaviour. The IMF similarly finds it difficult to provide funds on the requisite scale, given its limited resources relative to the size of the markets. Improved institutions and procedures could help to overcome these problems, facilitating the injection of new funds where an orderly restructuring of existing debts is not enough and the problem is clearly the ability rather than the willingness of the debtor to pay.

Inadequate crisis management. The appropriate role of creditor-country governments and the International Monetary Fund in managing such crises remains unclear. The Fund and the US government responded to the Mexican crisis in an *ad hoc* fashion that is unlikely to be repeated in the future. Although G–7 leaders agreed at the June 1995 Halifax Summit to double the General Arrangements to Borrow and to establish a new emergency financing mechanism to deal with Mexico-like problems, how the resources of that facility should be used remains unclear. Appropriate management roles for national governments and multilateral institutions have not been defined.

Inadequate crisis prevention. While everyone agrees on the desirability of preventing crises in the first place, there is no consensus on how this might be done. Improved policies are always desirable, but it may be possible for crises to occur even where policies are broadly appropriate (see section 2 below). The IMF has begun to engage in closer monitoring of economic conditions and issue sterner warnings of impending difficulties; the problem is that public warnings might only excite the markets and provoke the very crises that officials are concerned to head off.

In the wake of the Mexican crisis a number of proposals have appeared that address these concerns. Recommendations include promoting changes in the provisions of loan contracts and bond covenants; government support for the creation of bondholders' steering committees; expanding the signalling and mediation roles of the IMF; creating a venue for negotiations involving bondholders' representatives, the government of the indebted country and the IMF; and closing the courts of creditor countries to dissident creditors by statute or treaty. One prominent proposal (Sachs, 1995) is to establish a bankruptcy procedure for sovereign debtors analogous to Chapter 11 of the US bankruptcy code, which allows a company's creditors to petition for liquidation or reorganization.[3] Bankruptcy procedures under national law consist of three elements: the suspension of individual actions seeking to enforce debt claims against an enterprise; the negotiation of a plan to restructure the debt and to reorganize or liquidate the firm; and implementation of that plan. Substituting 'country' for 'firm' or 'enterprise' gives the proposal for a Chapter 11 for highly indebted, illiquid nations.

Given its high visibility, we consider this proposal in detail. In addition, we analyse the other approaches to reforming arrangements for dealing with sovereign financial crises, ranging from modest incremental reforms to a wholesale restructuring of the international lending process.

We find that there are problems with each of these schemes for institutional reform. In particular, it is unrealistic to envisage the creation of an international bankruptcy court empowered to supervise the restructuring process and impose agreed terms on dissident creditors. It is equally unrealistic to assume that the IMF can be given such powers. But this does not mean that limited reform is infeasible. We therefore offer a limited agenda for reform that includes encouraging the organization of bondholders' representative organs and creating a framework for parallel negotiations between the debtor government on the one hand and creditor governments, creditor banks and the bondholders' representative committee on the other. It includes encouraging the IMF to take a more active role in sanctioning or censuring countries that impose unilateral standstills and in providing information to all parties. It entails the creation of an agency that would facilitate the exchange of information and provide conciliation and (non-binding) arbitration services. It extends to efforts on the part of governments and multilateral organizations to promote reform-friendly innovations in the provisions of debt contracts.

Several of these proposals resemble ideas that were floated during the debt crisis of the 1980s. It is important, therefore, to say a few words about the types of countries to which these procedures would apply. This debt crisis gave rise to complaints about the cost of negotiations, the length of time required for their completion, the problems of achieving agreement on debt writedowns and the difficulty of injecting new money. In so far as these same difficulties arise today, even though the intermediation mechanism has shifted from bank towards bond and equity finance, the procedures sketched here should have some applicability to the entire spectrum of heavily indebted nations.[4] But they are especially relevant to countries whose debt takes the form of widely held, highly liquid, foreign-currency-denominated bonds. As the Mexican crisis reminds us, this is a new condition (for the post-second world war period) to which our procedures should be specially tailored.

The remainder of this report is organized as follows. Section 2 analyses the structure and rationale of national bankruptcy codes and the analogy with sovereign debt. Whatever people think of proposals for a bankruptcy procedure for sovereign debtors, the theory of bankruptcy helps them to identify the market failures and thus the economic functions of an efficient procedure for restructuring sovereign debts. We therefore start with some basic principles of bankruptcy theory. Section 3 contrasts theory with practice, describing the evolution of procedures used to deal with sovereign debt crises. This historical perspective sheds light on the argument that market solutions will evolve to meet the difficulties created by new financial structures; this is particularly relevant in view of the shift from bank lending to sovereign countries in the 1970s and the 1980s towards the kind of bond financing that was also prevalent in the inter-war period and the nineteenth century. Section 4 introduces the various proposals for enhancing the efficiency with which contracts are written *ex ante* and debt crises are managed *ex post*, ranging from modest incremental solutions to ambitious schemes that would apply the bankruptcy analogy closely. Section 5 evaluates the alternative proposals, and section 6 concludes.

2   Bankruptcy in theory and practice

The fundamental difference between a sovereign state and a firm is the public interest in maintaining a country as a going, indeed a well-functioning concern. We care about countries more – and in a different way – than we do about companies. Neither the international authorities, nor sensible creditor governments, nor private investors will wish to see a country's financial crisis lead to an economic and political crisis. But the economic analysis of procedures for maintaining distressed sovereign debtors as well-functioning economies with reasonable future prospects should start from the analysis of financial distress for firms.

In the corporate setting, debtors and creditors are not simply left to work out their financial difficulties on their own. A juridical tribunal or court provides what is, in effect, binding arbitration of their claims. Bankruptcy theory can help us to understand why this is the case and to think about whether the rationale carries over to sovereign debt.

If information were complete, contracts were perfectly enforceable and negotiating costs were negligible, there would be no need for a bankruptcy procedure (Cornelli and Felli, 1995). The contracting parties could specify the relevant contingencies and enforce the provisions applicable to the relevant outcomes. Were they to find themselves in a situation for which they had not made provision, they could recontract directly and arrive at an efficient outcome, provided property rights were clearly defined.

Complete information, costless contract enforcement and negligible negotiating costs are unrealistic assumptions. Bankruptcy procedures shift some of the risk created by the violation of these assumptions. It is difficult for parties to a transaction to forecast and provide for all the contingencies that may arise, for example. This may give rise to strategic behaviour among the contracting parties, leading to delay in reaching a negotiated settlement and to wasteful dissipation of resources. This is an example of the kind of market failure underlying arguments for a bankruptcy procedure to expedite negotiations.

It can be argued that debt contracts do not really make sense when they omit to mention the word 'default' and fail to specify an insolvency process, as is typical of sovereign debt. Think of a corporate debt contract that did not specify what happened in the event of default: it is hard to imagine that the interest rate would be lower as a result of this uncertainty. Imagine now a debt contract with an individual that did not allow for bankruptcy; this is called debt peonage or even slavery. In practice, corporate debt contracts normally include provisions for dealing with default, in consonance with the relevant national bankruptcy code. Private debt contracts are signed in the knowledge that defaults will be adjudicated by specific courts.

An efficient bankruptcy code balances two objectives: it seeks to maximize the *ex-post* value of the firm, and it attempts to encourage adherence to the *ex-ante* provisions of debt contracts (to preserve the bonding role of debt, in other words) by penalizing debtors for resorting to bankruptcy. A well-designed debt restructuring procedure for sovereign debt would similarly achieve a balance between these objectives. It would enhance the *ex-post* income and growth prospects of the debtor country, rescheduling debt service and, where necessary, clearing away an overhang of unserviceable debt by imposing agreed settlement terms on dissident creditors; and it would promote injection of new funds by granting seniority to new money where appropriate. But to avoid undermining the *ex-ante* bonding role of debt and discouraging lending, it would also have to include measures to reassure potential lenders that adherence to the terms of loan contracts would be strengthened in the future.

An efficient procedure preserves promising enterprises and liquidates uneconomic ones. Firms that are illiquid but not insolvent require only temporary protection from creditors, with no debt writedown. Insolvent firms that can earn their cost of capital after reorganization should be preserved; those which cannot should be liquidated. This means not only avoiding the premature liquidation of viable concerns and providing new funds (possibly writing down debts) to maintain an insolvent but economically viable firm as an operating concern, but also avoiding unjustified postponement of the liquidation of unviable enterprises. (See Franks, Nyborg and Torous, 1995; and Aghion, Hart and Moore, 1992.) We now consider how these goals are achieved in theory and in practice.

2.1 Theory

First, an efficient bankruptcy procedure provides incentives for gathering and dispensing information. It will not be immediately evident to all observers whether the enterprise can earn its cost of capital. Determining whether this is the case, and hence whether the firm should be liquidated or reorganized, requires gathering information. When creditors and others have complex and conflicting claims they may not view it as in their interest to share such facts. And if investors are risk averse, inadequate information may create a bias towards premature liquidation. When there is uncertainty about the extent and validity of creditors' claims, strategic bargaining in an environment of asymmetric information may cause considerable delay in concluding negotiations. An efficient bankruptcy procedure enables the court to induce the parties to share information. It may require the creditors to choose from a menu of writedowns and new funds as a way of revealing information. It may organize an auction of the firm through which expectations of future profitability can be revealed.

Second, an efficient bankruptcy procedure prevents a 'grab race' by creditors. Premature liquidation is averted by a standstill (in the case of the US Bankruptcy Code, by the 'Automatic Stay' provision), preventing creditors from pressing claims incurred before the initiation of bankruptcy proceedings. If the firm had a single creditor which ascertained that the enterprise could earn more than its cost of capital if reorganized, that creditor and management could negotiate the reorganization without risking premature liquidation and requiring judicial intervention. In practice, there are many creditors with conflicting claims, each of which has an incentive to secure its debt by attaching the firm's assets and leaving to other creditors the task of reorganization. The grab race provoked by this collective-action problem is averted by the Automatic Stay.

Third, an efficient bankruptcy procedure leads to the implementation of a reorganization plan. Once it is determined that the enterprise can earn at least the cost of capital when reorganized, a reorganization plan must still be implemented. This may entail choosing a new ownership structure as well as restructuring the firm's operations. It may require relieving the enterprise of a debt burden it cannot pay in order to restore it to health.

Fourth, an efficient bankruptcy procedure encourages adherence to the terms of debt contracts. The function of contracts is to solve problems of incentive compatibility and opportunism that would otherwise prevent mutually desirable transactions. Agents allocate resources on the expectation that contracts will be enforced and that the priority of claims will be respected. If the bankruptcy process provides creditors with strong incentives to surrender their claims, they may be reluctant to enter into debt contracts in the first place. Modifications that are efficient *ex post* may lead to outcomes that are inefficient *ex ante*. An efficient bankruptcy procedure should balance *ex-post* efficiency (enhancing the efficiency with which a firm operates by lightening its debt load, for example) against *ex-ante* efficiency (encouraging future lending by strictly enforcing the provisions of current contracts, for instance).

Fifth, an efficient bankruptcy procedure encourages efficient levels of investment. Conflicts among creditors or between creditors and debtors may cause viable investment opportunities to go unexploited. The creditors may be unable to agree on the extent to which their claims should be written down. Incomplete information may give some of them leverage with which to hold up the reorganization process. Investors may be deterred from injecting new funds by the fear of being 'taxed' to pay old creditors. Bankruptcy codes therefore feature non-unanimity voting rules, so that only a majority of creditors in the UK administration procedure, or a majority of creditors in each class in the US and Japanese cases, need approve a reorganization plan. Chapter 11 makes provision for 'cramdown', in which the court may force a non-assenting class of creditors to accept only the amount they would have obtained in liquidation.[5]

An efficient bankruptcy code prevents not only under-investment but over-investment as well. A code which limits the losses incurred by equity holders truncates the lower tail of the distribution of returns, effectively giving equity holders a free call option on the firm. This encourages excessive investment, which is socially inefficient (Sussman, 1994).

Sixth, an efficient bankruptcy procedure protects other stakeholder interests. An enterprise may generate social surplus that accrues to agents other than management and shareholders in the firm itself. It may generate productivity spillovers to other firms. Its existence may reduce costs for firms which use the intermediate products it supplies in ways that are not captured by the upstream firm (Rodrik, 1995a). It may be a source of rents to workers who earn more than the marginal productivity of labour. Measures to encourage its survival may encourage workers to invest in firm-specific human capital (Shleifer and Summers, 1988). These 'private benefits' that are not internalized by management and creditors are taken into account in an efficient bankruptcy proceeding (Franks and Nyborg, 1994).

The benefits to stakeholders in the bankrupt company must be balanced, however, against costs imposed on stakeholders in other companies. Such costs can arise, for example, if bankruptcy is used strategically to secure a competitive advantage. Bankruptcy may force concessions on a firm's unionized labour force or allow the bankrupt firm to raise new funds at rates that cannot be obtained by competitors who, for whatever reason, cannot take recourse to protection against existing creditors.

Seventh, an efficient bankruptcy procedure encourages innovations in the structure of debt contracts. As monitoring and negotiating technologies evolve, so too do the provisions of efficient contracts. An inflexible, bureaucratic bankruptcy code that encourages adherence to the terms of debt contracts, protects stakeholder interests and delivers other results at the cost of stifling contractual and procedural innovation will be dynamically inefficient.

Eighth, an efficient bankruptcy procedure minimizes direct insolvency costs. A procedure which preserves promising enterprises and liquidates uneconomic ones only at the cost of substantial dissipation of resources (attorneys' fees, accountants' fees, etc.) involves an efficiency loss to society. Minimizing direct costs requires flexible and efficient administration of the law and expeditious decision-making.

An efficient bankruptcy procedure encourages parties to renegotiate contracts and reorganize the enterprise on their own. This requires even-handed protection of the rights of debtors and creditors, since a bankruptcy procedure which favours one party too strongly will induce it both to reject offers tendered outside court and to litigate. Whether and how the assets of the enterprise can be seized by the court-appointed administrator and whether incumbent management can be penalized or replaced should be governed by the desire to encourage sincere and speedy negotiations (Cornelli and Felli, 1995).

2.2   Domestic practice

Different national bankruptcy codes attempt to achieve the goals enumerated above in very different ways. Indeed, one of the central conclusions of our analysis is that there are very great differences among national bankruptcy codes. These suggest such fundamentally different perspectives that it seems highly unlikely that the relevant governments could be induced to line up behind any version of a Chapter 11 procedure. This need not preclude agreement on less comprehensive measures that reduce the likelihood that a debt workout will be required and promote an orderly workout when it is, but it cautions against applying the Chapter 11 analogy mechanically.

For example, whereas a reorganized firm may assign administrative priority to the repayment of new loans in the United States, in the United Kingdom priority for new funds is possible only with the permission of existing creditors, which is rarely granted in practice. The ease with which priority is granted to new funds in the United States may encourage excessive investment, while the UK receivership code is criticized for leading to under-investment. Even under Chapter 11, 'debtor in possession' financing with 'supra-priority' is not as automatic as sometimes suggested; it requires the agreement of the court and cannot impair the collateral of the claims of most secured debt.

The German insolvency code currently in force provides for a three-month mandatory moratorium (and an unlimited stay against unsecured creditors), and the court-appointed insolvency administrator can raise new senior financing. Under-investment may still be a problem, however, because secured creditors can take possession of their assets, and secured claims account for the vast majority of claims against German firms. A reformed bankruptcy code, which will come into operation in 1999, eliminates many of the special prerogatives of secured creditors. Secured and unsecured creditors will still vote separately on the reorganization plan, acceptance requiring simple majority by count and claim in each group.

In the United Kingdom the receiver is liable for all additional debts incurred after the date of his appointment; this is an obvious disincentive to raising further funds relative to the US system, where liability falls on the firm rather than the court-appointed trustee. The receiver is encouraged to come to a quick decision regarding the viability of the enterprise, raising the risk of premature liquidation.[6] Since the 1986 Insolvency Act it has also been possible to appoint an administrator rather than a receiver, where the administrator is not personally responsible for liabilities incurred after his appointment. The administration procedure offers a three-month automatic stay.

The tendency under the US code is to encourage the maintenance of companies as going concerns even when it is in the interests of creditors and society for them to be liquidated. The free call option effectively granted to shareholders (who gain if the value of the firm rises but whose losses are bounded below because of limited liability) encourages an extended period of reorganization, since a longer period generally increases the probability that the value of the firm, and hence the value of the option, will rise. Management and the court cannot be compelled to liquidate even when the firm is worth less in continued operation. In contrast, German and UK creditors can force the administrator to liquidate.

The US code gives power and value to the debtor in possession in the hope that the actions of shareholder management will be consonant with the interests of indirect stakeholders. In practice, however, the interests of the debtor in possession and other stakeholders may not coincide. Chapter 11 is said to jeopardize the preservation of debt contracts by upsetting the priority of claims. It gives strong protection to the debtor in possession, favouring shareholders over debtholders (Franks and Torous, 1989; Weiss, 1990; Jensen, 1992). The UK receivership code, in contrast, maintains the priority of claims, although unsecured creditors may be disadvantaged relative to secured creditors.

The judicial authority is very active, indeed interventionist, under Chapter 11. The debtor in possession must report to the court on a continuing basis and ask permission for any major sales, investments, etc.; creditors are often consulted before the judge gives a decision.

The United Kingdom deals with moral hazard – the temptation for management to pursue strategies which increase the likelihood of having to renege on the firm's debt obligations subsequently – by forcing the board of directors to relinquish control when a receiver or administrator is appointed. A similar approach is used in Germany, where initiation of an insolvency procedure entails replacing management. In the United States, in contrast, management often maintains control throughout reorganization. Only when the firm enters liquidation is management compelled to step down.

The US code is relatively flexible and conducive to change. In recent years this evolution has in practice reflected the perceived high costs to creditors of actually going into Chapter 11. So bankruptcy has been 'privatized', in the form of increasingly prevalent workouts: that is, exchanges of securities of financially distressed firms outside the formal bankruptcy process. The same incentives have led to pre-packaged Chapter 11s, in which a reorganization plan is arranged outside the formal bankruptcy procedure and submitted to a vote in Chapter 11 only to take advantage of non-unanimity provisions. Note that writedowns of debt in Chapter 11 average 51% but in workouts only 20% – the more solvent firms avoid Chapter 11 – and the workout process averages 17 months in duration, whereas Chapter 11 proceedings average 27 months (Franks and Torous, 1994).

Out of court proceedings are also used in the United Kingdom and Germany, although they are less prevalent. The fact that a small number of banks act as large lenders to business and therefore control the bankruptcy process in these countries may allow them to place barriers against the evolution of debt contracts.

Different national insolvency codes have different reputations for administrative efficiency. In the German system the administrator's compensation is partly a function of time. This provides an incentive for the administrator to drag out liquidation. Under the US system, where lawyers' fees can be a function of the duration of the liquidation/reorganization process, Chapter 11 is criticized for its lengthiness; LoPucki and Whitford (1992) report that large bankruptcies spend an average of up to three years in Chapter 11. Direct bankruptcy costs have been estimated to average 3% of the book value of debts plus pre-bankruptcy equity (Weiss, 1990). In the UK code the receiver is not obliged to report to the court (unless he is court-appointed), so reducing administrative costs.

These comparisons reveal very considerable differences in the structure and operation of national codes. In particular, the balance between debtor and creditor interests is significantly more favourable to the former under Chapter 11 than in the United Kingdom or Germany, a fact that will condition national attitudes towards proposals for sovereign bankruptcy procedures. Moreover, even proponents of an international Chapter 11 must recognize that Chapter 11 is seriously criticized in the United States for its high costs and, perhaps more importantly for our purposes, the wide discretion for *ex-post* changes in debt contracts, which some regard as *ex-ante* inefficient.

2.3　Bankruptcy in the sovereign setting

In what respects are the circumstances of financially distressed sovereign debtors similar to those of illiquid or insolvent firms, so that the features of an efficient domestic bankruptcy code might apply to countries? While there is no relevant sense in which a country, unlike an enterprise, can be closed down or reorganized, finance ministers are more vulnerable; and the distinction between illiquidity and insolvency has an analogue in the literature on sovereign debt.[7] But the solvency of a country is not well defined, since it is difficult to distinguish between its ability to pay and its willingness to pay. The present value of GDP may far exceed debt, but it may not be politically acceptable (or economically justifiable) to divert output from domestic use (consumption and investment) to net exports sufficiently to meet debt service obligations. (We develop this point below in the context of our discussion of self-fulfilling debt crises.) Thus there may be arguments for debt forgiveness even if on some calculations the country is 'solvent'.

This points to a key problem that arises when thinking about the financial reorganization of a country, namely the lack of an analogue for the value of the firm. In corporate reorganization the value of the firm may be transparent, because for example its assets are sold, or it may not, because for example the value of the firm's intangible assets is difficult to appraise, but either way the creditors will receive new securities in the reorganized company. In contrast, when a country defaults there are fundamental ambiguities in assessing the value of the underlying assets. This makes it particularly difficult for creditors to agree to a restructuring that in effect promises them 'equity in the reorganized company'. This absence of any analogue to the value of the firm may be interpreted as the lack, for creditors, of a well-specified outside option (such as the liquidation value) which would determine their bargaining power; hence it affects the negotiation process in an essential way.

The introduction of an IMF programme with tough conditionality can be thought of as analogous to the replacement of management in domestic bankruptcy. Although the government will normally remain in place, its control over domestic policies is often severely restricted. The threat of this loss of control may in turn be a deterrent to behaviour that might lead to financial distress.

The assumption of incomplete information that justifies recourse to bankruptcy is certainly applicable to sovereign debt. It is difficult for creditors to assemble information about the financial prospects of the country to whose debt they have claims and to verify the accuracy of information released by its government. It is difficult to verify the government's assertions of political strength and the extent of public support for the policies necessary for the maintenance of debt service. The asymmetry of information between debtor and creditor is indeed typically stronger for a sovereign debtor than a corporate debtor; and the large number of creditors exacerbates the free-rider problem that makes any individual creditor exercise too little monitoring of the debtor. The implication is that debt contracts are incomplete, and negotiations are costly. This provides a rationale for efficiency-enhancing intervention.

The desirability of encouraging adherence to the terms of loan contracts carries over from the corporate to the sovereign setting; the repudiation or modification of contracts would discourage lending to countries in the same way that it deters lending to corporations. There is a clear case for new money for a country meeting the conditions for financing rather than forgiving a debt overhang (Krugman, 1988). And there is the same problem of achieving this in a setting where new creditors are deterred from lending because they fear being 'taxed' by old creditors. Thus granting priority to post-bankruptcy debt is desirable if the implications for moral hazard can be contained. Protecting other stakeholder interests is analogous to ensuring that the government can continue to carry out its basic functions: providing law enforcement, public order, a stable currency and basic social protection. As with corporate bankruptcy, it is desirable to minimize the dissipation of resources by negotiation.

Most national bankruptcy procedures empower a court-appointed trustee to act as arbiter in disputes over restructuring packages. (In some cases the bankruptcy court itself assumes this role.) It can be costly for particular creditors to dispute the findings of the court with regard to, *inter alia*, the prospective revenues of the reorganized enterprise. This function carries over to the sovereign setting, where the IMF provides a 'seal of approval' to debtors' projections of economic variables.[8]

There is, however, a key difference that impedes coordination and underlies the collective action problem in the sovereign debtor case. In domestic bankruptcy there is an obvious jurisdiction. An agreement between a country and foreign private creditors is normally subject to a specified system of national law, 'the proper law of the contract'. This is likely to differ among a sovereign borrower's various debt contracts. Thus in the case of a distressed sovereign debtor, one essential feature of domestic bankruptcy law is absent: there is no court system with jurisdiction over the totality of the debtor state's obligations which can thereby compel dissident creditors to accept a generally agreed restructuring. Commercial bankruptcy, in contrast, occurs within the framework of a single legal system.[9]

Empirical evidence suggests that for the markets, the key issue is indeed whose law governs: for example, spreads on Italian bonds issued in Rome are virtually identical, whether they are denominated in ECUs or in lire; whereas spreads on Italian bonds issued in New York are very much lower than on those issued in Rome in the same currency (Favero, Giavazzi and Spaventa, 1995). The markets assume that if the government has to default, it will do so on domestic debt but not on the debt that is registered in New York, because the legal complications there would be more trouble than they would be worth.

All national bankruptcy codes provide for at least a limited standstill to contain the scope for a damaging creditor 'grab race' for the firm's assets. A sovereign debtor can equally suffer adverse consequences when its creditors rush for the exits. Here the key issue is not the seizure of assets (as we point out in section 4.2, this is unlikely to be a serious problem) but rather the rush to grab foreign exchange reserves by selling domestic currency or redeeming foreign-currency obligations issued by the government or domestic firms.

The argument is based on the model of self-fulfilling debt runs (Calvo, 1988). Assume a government which can maintain service on its debts as long as its creditors renew their maturing obligations. In the absence of expectations of substantial redemptions, each creditor is willing to renew maturing obligations. But if the number of creditors refusing to roll over their maturing obligations reaches a critical threshold, the government will lack the resources needed to redeem them and also maintain service on its other debts. In this setting a run on the debt can be self-fulfilling. There can exist two equilibria, one in which the government defaults and one in which it does not. Even if all creditors are better off when they roll over their maturing issues, allowing the government to keep current service on its debts, the suspicion that some creditors will be tempted to redeem their maturing issues may cause other creditors to attempt to get out first, leading to a self-fulfilling run. The creditors as a class may be worse off, since only those who sell prior to default recover their principal, while the government will be worse off in so far as it incurs costs of default (which damage its reputation, jeopardize its credit market access, etc.). Yet the collective action problem facing the creditors may prevent them from coordinating on the more desirable equilibrium. Hence the grab-run analogy.

Schwartz (1995) questions whether there can exist self-fulfilling debt runs on the same grounds that some economists question the idea of self-fulfilling bank runs. Models of self-fulfilling bank runs are driven by the assumption that the act of liquidating assets itself involves a cost that reduces the value of the bank's loan portfolio; in this case, runs need not depend on any prior loss in the value of the assets that underlie deposits (Diamond and Dybvig, 1983). An objection to this assumption is that banks also possess capital which can be drawn upon to finance deposit withdrawals and which thereby reassures depositors. Banks which suffer runs, in this view, are those which mismanage their loan portfolios, not those which experience arbitrary shifts between multiple equilibria.

By analogy, countries possess resources with the same effect as bank capital. It is within their capacity to raise taxes if this is required to reassure their creditors; the knowledge that this is so should enable governments to access international capital. Governments which fall prey to financial crises are those which mismanage their monetary and fiscal affairs.

Ultimately, then, the analogy rests on the realism of the assumption that countries have the political and economic flexibility to raise taxes and impose the other measures of austerity needed to reassure their creditors. The argument of Sachs (1995) is that such measures may jeopardize support for the government, which will therefore hesitate to pursue them. Hence there is a danger of self-fulfilling debt runs and a need for bankruptcy-like procedures to provide an automatic stay, a cramdown, a reorganization and new funds.

Some economists and officials remain unconvinced. Our view is that an effective stay will sometimes be essential because markets can move too quickly to leave time for the government to push through the national legislature the painful fiscal measures needed to reassure panicked investors or even to get IMF approval of a package of new policies; and because a run may threaten a fragile banking system that cannot be strengthened overnight, with damaging political as well as economic consequences. The policy-making community clearly subscribes to the view that governments can be severely constrained by domestic political conditions in how they respond to crises. This introduces the danger that crises can erupt even in the absence of serious underlying policy imbalances: that is, they can give rise to a self-fulfilling 'run' that is not justified by – or forecastable in terms of – economic 'fundamentals'. That is a clear market failure.

Whether this requires a full-blown bankruptcy procedure for sovereign debtors is a separate question. We maintain below that arguments from bankruptcy theory and the analogy between corporate financial distress and sovereign debtor distress are sufficient to justify the following features of corporate workouts in the sovereign context: some form of temporary 'stay' procedure to block the 'rush for the exits'; provision *ex ante* for the possibility that stretchouts and writedowns may become necessary; and measures for dealing with the problem of dissident creditors in the context of a restructuring plan that commands wide assent. Nevertheless, there are compelling objections to schemes for achieving these ends through a 'sovereign bankruptcy procedure'.

This point is underscored by the substantial differences in national bankruptcy codes that we outlined in section 2.2; the analogy between domestic and sovereign distressed debtors will appear different in the light of different national bankruptcy codes. Receivership of the sort practised in the United Kingdom, where a representative of the creditor with the floating charge obtains control of the company, is clearly not feasible in the sovereign context, for example. Procedures that contain moral hazard by replacing management, as in the United Kingdom and Germany, have only limited applicability in so far as there is a parallel in the form of IMF conditionality. The power of secured creditors to seize collateral varies across countries, and there are clear questions about whether bankruptcy procedures which rely on the bonding role of collateral have any practical application to sovereign debt (see section 4.2 below). The question, then, is whether it is possible to design a procedure that does not rely on these features of bankruptcy codes.

3 The evolution of procedures for renegotiating sovereign debts

Critics of a bankruptcy procedure for indebted countries argue that creditors and debtors, faced with a Mexico-style problem, can negotiate an efficient solution by themselves. Intervention by creditor-country governments or an international bankruptcy court will only disrupt the process. As Schwartz (1995, p. 10) writes of the recent episode: 'Mexico should not be the ward of the United States. Mexico should have negotiated with tesobono holders a stretchout and a writedown of those maturing debts. The creditors would have formed a committee to represent them in the negotiations. The government should have announced a plan to deal with bank insolvencies, a plan to adjust its monetary policies, and a commitment to reduce the inflation rate.'

Historical experience is a source of evidence on whether bargaining between debtors and creditors yields efficient outcomes. It addresses the question of whether the markets, left to themselves, will develop adequate institutional arrangements for coping with crises.

3.1 Bondholders' representative committees

Experience with fixed-interest debt from the nineteenth century to the 1930s is particularly relevant to the issues at hand, given the prominence of fixed-interest securities in today's international capital markets. One popular proposal for reform is the resuscitation of bondholders' representative committees. To understand whether this makes sense and how they might be structured, it is important to review their history.

In the nineteenth century, as today, bond markets mediated investment in emerging markets. When financial crises struck, governments might halt investors' rush for the exits by unilaterally suspending debt service payments and, in some cases, imposing exchange controls. Bond finance meant that there were many small investors in the securities of governments, heightening free-rider problems and negotiating costs. Significant institutional innovations sprang up in response to these difficulties. Bondholders represented themselves in negotiations with sovereign debtors by forming committees (Eichengreen and Portes, 1989a). At first, self-standing, self-liquidating committees were established to negotiate individual defaults with individual debtors. Competing committees proliferated in the United Kingdom and other creditor countries. They solicited subscriptions from bondholders and attempted to negotiate settlement terms with the debtor. When the committee announced that the debtor had negotiated in good faith and endorsed its offer as the best that could be expected, bondholders were asked to validate the agreement by registering their opinion with the committee or by cashing a coupon with the debtor. Bondholders dissatisfied by the offer could continue to hold out for better terms, but they had little leverage, especially if the representative committee's endorsement of the offer permitted organized trading in the securities of the foreign government to resume.

In the United Kingdom this situation was regularized by the creation of the Corporation of Foreign Bondholders (CFB) in 1868. Initially the Council, the Corporation's governing body, comprised representatives of banking firms and brokerage houses. In 1898 it was reorganized by an act of Parliament which removed the representatives of the issue houses and expanded the Council to include several substantial bondholders and a representative of the London Chamber of Commerce.

The creation of a permanent entity is credited with reducing operating costs. It prevented debtors from playing off one committee against another. It is noteworthy that this evolution occurred largely on private impetus. While the UK government welcomed the emergence of the CFB, which received semi-official status in the form of a parliamentary charter, government officials did little to support the CFB in negotiations. The government's hands-off attitude was summarized by Lord Palmerston's remark that 'His Majesty's Government is not a debt collector'.

The CFB's bargaining power derived from its ability to work closely with the London issue houses and the stock exchange. Under the provisions of a rule adopted in 1825, the stock exchange prohibited quotations in the securities of a country in default on its bonded debt which had refused to negotiate in good faith. For information on the status of loans and readjustment negotiations, the stock exchange came to rely on the CFB. Thus the CFB's endorsement of a settlement, by lifting this ban, held out the promise of reviving capital market access.

In the United States the same evolution occurred, albeit with delay. The first significant US protective committee, the Committee on Foreign Securities, was formed in 1918 (a short-lived and insignificant predecessor having died in the 1870s). But an organization comparable to the Corporation of Foreign Bondholders (the Foreign Bondholders Protective Council, or FBPC) was established only in the mid-1930s, reflecting the late emergence of the United States as a creditor nation.

Until then bondholders relied on *ad-hoc* committees which suffered from high administrative expenses and lacked the reputation and authority to negotiate effectively. Competing committees circled around defaulted bonds 'like vultures gathering around bones' (Sessions, 1992, p. 22). By 1934 there were some 40 committees in the United States. The FBPC was therefore created with the encouragement of the State Department. Its operating expenses were met by contributions by US financial institutions. As in the United Kingdom in the nineteenth century, negotiations proceeded with a minimum of government involvement.[10]

Thus negotiation between debtors and creditors, with little intervention by creditor-country governments, was relied upon to clear up the legacy of sovereign defaults in the era of bond finance. Governments which defaulted on their debts reached negotiated settlements with their creditors; cases like Czarist debts renounced by the former Soviet Union that remained in default for more than two-thirds of a century were exceptions to the rule, driven by a society's decision to repudiate not just its debts but the market system as a whole.

The terms secured by the creditors, while less favourable than those initially offered in the bond covenant, were not disastrous. While the *ex-ante* rate of return offered on foreign bonds compared favourably with the yield on US or UK government securities, the *ex-post* return, though somewhat lower, was positive for most bond issues that lapsed into default. Eichengreen and Portes (1989b) found that the nominal internal rate of return on foreign dollar bonds issued in the 1920s was 4%, and on sterling bonds 5%. By comparison, *ex-ante* returns were in the range of 7–8%. Lindert and Morton (1990) found that lending to ten major sovereign borrowers gave a real rate of return of 2.1% in 1850–1914 and 3.8% for loans extended in the inter-war period – in both cases the rate exceeded by over 1% the domestic (sterling or dollar) government bond real return. Klingen (1995) studies bank lending to sovereign countries between 1970 and 1992 and finds an average nominal rate of return of 8% (1.9% below the average Libor) and an average real rate of 2.1%. Thus across a long historical sweep, with many defaults and reschedulings and under a variety of different institutional arrangements, the average *ex-post* real rate of return on lending to sovereigns has remained remarkably similar: about 2–3%, not much different from that on 'riskless' lending.[11]

Typically, a negotiated solution took years to conclude. In the worst cases, like the 1820s and the 1930s, the better part of two decades was required for negotiations to erase the legacy of sovereign default (Bolivia, the first country to default, in 1931, was the last to settle, in 1958). In the nineteenth century, when a solution was reached and a country signalled that it had put its domestic financial house in order (generally by adopting the measures necessary to go onto the gold standard – see Fishlow, 1989) it was again able to float bond issues. Thus all of the major nineteenth century defaulters were able to re-enter the capital market following settlement.

The outcome following the more pervasive defaults of the 1930s was less satisfactory: the market for foreign government bonds remained largely dormant after the second world war. Significant international flows of portfolio capital resumed only with the relaxation of capital controls and institutional innovation in the form of bank finance in the 1960s.[12]

These complaints can be understood in terms of bankruptcy theory – in particular, in terms of the conditions under which no third-party intervention is justified on efficiency grounds. For direct bargaining between debtor and creditors to produce an efficient outcome, the creditors' rush for the exits must be avoided. In fact, unilateral action by a sovereign government can produce an approximation to an automatic stay, in so far as it is difficult for foreign creditors to seize assets of a government that unilaterally suspends debt service payments.[13] But subsequent bargaining will produce an efficient solution only if information is symmetric. In practice, bondholders were imperfectly informed about the preferences and strength of governments and the costs facing them. Debt negotiations could take on a war-of-attrition character, where both parties utilized delay to elicit information about the cost-bearing capacity of their counterpart. Different classes of creditors had complex and conflicting claims; those who had subscribed to stabilization loans endorsed by the League of Nations claimed priority over investors in other bonds. Negotiations between bondholders and governments lacked a mechanism for dealing with dissident creditors. Moreover, there was no international court with jurisdiction over debtor governments that failed to bargain in good faith. The 'full faith and credit' provisions of the bond covenant could not be enforced except in the courts of the debtor country itself, and then only if the government was willing to waive its sovereign immunity. Even if a judgment was made against a government, there was no legal machinery with which to enforce it.

Overall, experience with market-driven negotiations in the earlier era of bond finance paints a mixed picture. The markets did develop arrangements – bondholders' committees and bilateral negotiations – for restructuring defaulted debts. But in both the United States and the United Kingdom, the authority of the committee rested on official recognition by the State Department or Parliament.

These committees fulfilled useful functions. But the mere existence of a representative body for creditors did not obviate the need for governments to resort to unilateral standstills. It is sometimes argued that the inter-war experience is irrelevant because the increase in size and speed of reaction of international capital markets and the overall globalization of finance have created a qualitatively different environment. But in the inter-war period too, the markets reacted quickly and forced the hand of governments. Moreover, there was evident contagion in the wave of defaults that swept through Latin America in 1931 and Europe in 1932 (Eichengreen and Portes, 1987).

Committees were rarely if ever able to negotiate a restructuring before the suspension of debt service payments. It is not hard to see why: news of those negotiations would have led to the collapse of bond prices and only exacerbated the government's difficulties. While negotiated solutions were eventually reached – dissident creditors might continue to press their case, but they had little leverage – settlement often required an extended period of negotiations during which the creditors received no income, the debtor enjoyed no capital market access, and all parties complained of the wasteful dissipation of resources in unproductive negotiations. While debtors were eventually able to re-enter the market and creditors were willing to resume lending, bondholders' committees were no panacea.[14]

3.2   The Paris Club

With the breakdown of international bond markets, intergovernmental loans became the conduit for portfolio capital flows after the second world war. Industrial-country governments, notably that of the United States, provided official credits (and guaranteed private-sector lending) to private- and public-sector borrowers in developing countries. As problems arose, the Paris Club procedures for rescheduling official credits were developed starting in the 1950s. It is worth asking how well the Paris Club procedures have worked in facilitating renegotiation and whether procedures which have been employed there to reschedule official credits have any applicability to bonded debt.

The Paris Club is an informal group of creditor governments operating according to an agreed set of policies and procedures. There is a permanent secretariat based at the French Treasury and a set of rules and guidelines (see below) by which it seeks to treat debtor countries consistently. 'Membership' varies by case. The first Paris Club negotiation took place in 1956, when Argentina agreed to meet in Paris with its official creditors to negotiate a rescheduling of payments due on officially supported export credits (Rieffel, 1985). By the mid-1960s discussions had coalesced around four conventions or principles that should be satisfied by any negotiated settlement.

Imminent default. To be eligible for a Paris Club rescheduling, it must be agreed that the debtor country is unable to meet its debt service obligations. The IMF functions as referee; its forecast of the balance-of-payments position of the country is used to establish the existence of this condition. This requirement can be thought of as preventing 'strategic bankruptcy'.

Appropriate conditionality. Since the second half of the 1960s the Paris Club has required the debtor to conclude an agreement with the IMF before commencing rescheduling negotiations. In terms of bankruptcy theory, this can be seen as ensuring that the country has an 'appropriate reorganization plan' in place. It minimizes the moral hazard that would arise if debt were restructured or written down without requiring the country to adopt at the same time new policies that constrain policy-makers and reduce the risk of a repetition of financial difficulties. Thus the IMF plays a major role behind the scenes in brokering the agreement between the debtor and its official creditors. The manner in which it has done so has varied over time; in the case of low-income countries, for example, the Club now recognizes not only stand-by agreements but also Fund authorization to draw on Structural Adjustment Facilities and Enhanced Structural Adjustment Facilities.

Equitable burden sharing. This principle embodies the idea that all creditors should participate in the debt relief operation. It applies to commercial banks and other private creditors in addition to official creditors. All credits of the same type are rescheduled with the same grace and repayment periods. Paris Club agreements include a 'non-discriminatory clause' which commits the debtor not to accept worse conditions from non-participating official creditors than from Paris Club members. The country is expected to seek debt relief from private creditors as generous as the official relief granted by the Paris Club ('comparable treatment'). The IMF and other multilateral agencies are exempt from equitable burden sharing (because they are regarded as preferred creditors), but they are expected to provide new money. These burden-sharing provisions can be interpreted as addressing free-rider problems which would otherwise prevent the injection of new funds, which would simply go to servicing the claims of the dissident creditors in the absence of burden sharing.

Consensus. Paris Club members must unanimously approve each element of a settlement. This is a departure from bankruptcy procedures like Chapter 11 in which it is necessary to obtain the assent only of a majority of creditors in each class. Majority rule and 'cramdown' are designed to prevent individual creditors from holding up the negotiation. It is striking, therefore, that hold-up does not appear to be a serious problem in the Paris Club, and it typically comes to a settlement more quickly than Chapter 11 proceedings. This speed is only relative, however; for example, the negotiations for Poland in 1990–1 went on for 15 months after the 1 January 1990 stabilization programme. (That the London Club took much longer, until November 1994, is also a relevant comparison.)

Implementing an agreement requires a bilateral agreement between the debtor and each creditor, as part of which the 'moratorium interest rate' is defined. These agreements typically require an additional six to eight months to conclude. The IMF may disburse new funds, however, as soon as the main Paris Club agreement is concluded.

Thus Paris Club negotiations resolve debt problems connected with official credits by employing principles that broadly resemble provisions in bankruptcy codes. The IMF plays a behind-the-scenes role in brokering the agreement. One important respect in which Paris Club procedures depart from commercial bankruptcy codes is in shunning majority voting rules and 'cramdown'. That only a handful, typically a dozen or so, creditor-country governments are involved and that these governments deal with one another repeatedly in a variety of different forums may discourage hold-up and non-cooperative behaviour. The governments involved tend to be those of the large OECD countries; consensus might be more difficult to build were large non-OECD creditors also involved.

This suggests that applying similar methods to the bond market will require the establishment of representative committees or other institutional devices to deal with large-numbers problems. Even with the establishment of bondholders' committees, however, it will be much more difficult to obtain the unanimous assent to a rescheduling from many thousands of bondholders engaged in a one-shot game than from a dozen creditor governments who interact repeatedly over time.

If this presumption is correct, there may be an argument for creating a debt tribunal or forum for negotiations between the government and the creditors, with the assistance of multilateral institutions. We explore these alternatives below. It may be undesirable, however, to transfer the activities of the Paris Club to this new forum, since the Club appears to carry out its tasks rather well. It would be better to coordinate negotiations over private credits in the new forum with the Paris Club's rescheduling of official debts.

3.3   The London Club

The London Club is a framework for rescheduling credits extended by commercial banks to governments, central banks and other public sector institutions.[15] Like its counterpart in Paris, it is a set of conventions rather than an institution. If anything it is even less formal; there is no fixed venue or continuing secretariat, but rather a body of agreed procedures and case law. As in the Paris Club, participation varies as a function of which commercial banks have exposure.

Much in the manner that bondholders formed representative committees, banks participating in London Club negotiations form a steering committee, typically with 15 members. Exposure and regional representation are taken into account when the composition of the committee is determined.

Again, the procedures of the London Club can be understood in terms of the basic principles of bankruptcy theory. As with official creditors, commercial banks have insisted on some form of 'IMF seal of approval' before conducting a restructuring.[16] Thus the IMF sets the stage for London Club negotiations by coordinating its agreement with the Paris Club. While London Club agreements also entail a 'non-discriminatory clause' committing the debtor not to extend more favourable treatment to dissident creditors than to London Club members, banks which have restructured their loans before the initiation of London Club negotiations can receive more favourable terms. Working in the other direction is the fact that sovereign bank loan agreements contain a provision, the 'sharing clause', requiring any creditor who receives a disproportionate payment from the debtor to share that payment with other creditors (Hurlock, 1995).

The London Club more closely resembles commercial bankruptcy in its use of agreement by consensus. Rather than requiring unanimity, as in the Paris Club, the agreement with the banks' steering committee need be approved only by banks holding up to 90–95% of total bank exposure. But nothing compels dissenting banks to go along; most loan agreements provide that each individual debt holder must consent to any amendment which has the effect of altering the terms of repayment of principal and interest. Creditors can sue sovereign debtors for enforcement of the terms of the original loan agreement. They can therefore hold up the process until they are bought out by the debtor or other creditors.[17] By the standards of the Paris Club, the London Club can thus take a lengthy period to conclude negotiations. This reflects the fact that similar procedures are more unwieldy when there are a large number of creditors. Typically, the banks on the steering committee must at each stage of defining the terms of an agreement get approval from all the banks they represent. And each is represented by different legal counsel who must scrutinize all new proposed agreements with the debtor. The efficiency of the process is open to question: it took Poland almost 14 years (from January 1981) to complete its debt restructuring, for example.

Turning from bank to bond finance, the experience of the London Club again points to the desirability of establishing an entity that can speak for the bondholders comparable to the steering committee that speaks for the banks. The comparison with the Paris Club suggests that effective representation becomes more difficult as the number of interested investors grows. It highlights the fact that measures which would permit a majority of bondholders to modify the terms of payment specified in the loan covenant would expedite the restructuring process. But in turn this raises the question of whether the bondholders themselves would feel sufficiently protected if provisions in loan agreements allowed the terms of repayment to be more easily modified. Would this not make them more reluctant to lend, raising the cost and reducing the availability of credit to developing countries? We consider these questions in the context of reviewing options for reform.

3.4   Managing the debt crisis of the 1980s

The Paris and London Clubs were the principal venues for negotiations between official and commercial bank creditors and the governments of developing countries when the debt crisis broke out in 1982. One conclusion that emerges from that experience is that the stance of the IMF and of the leading creditor-country governments could shift the balance of power in negotiations in ways that significantly affected the nature and timing of settlements.

As described above, an agreement with the IMF was taken as necessary to signal that effective policy reforms were in place; it was effectively a prerequisite for a negotiated settlement. As the commercial banks strengthened their balance sheet positions and the Brady Plan signalled the willingness of the major creditor-country governments to see the banks take losses, the IMF relaxed the conditions it attached to its own disbursements, heightening the pressure on the banks to settle. Until 1987–8 the IMF typically held up its own disbursements until a critical mass of commercial banks had agreed on new financing and debt restructuring. So long as the banks' balance sheets were weak, this served to pressure them to agree to concessions and come up with new money. But as the banks made provision for losses, they were less inclined to do so, and the Fund's policy of making its disbursements conditional on agreement with the banks worked to strengthen the bargaining position of the latter. Net IMF lending to Baker Plan countries declined significantly between 1983–5 and 1986–8, reflecting this tendency for the banks to hold multilateral funds hostage (Cline, 1989). Debt reduction and the provision of significant new money became difficult to engineer, as individual banks found themselves in a stronger position and each held out in the hope that others would agree to a writedown of their assets or to provide new funds (Helpman, 1988).

After 1987–8 the Fund took to making disbursements even when no agreement with the banks had been reached. It approved adjustment packages that involved less than full payment to the banks. The change in policy was authorized by the Executive Board. It shifted bargaining power from the banks to the debtor government and was a significant step towards the debt reduction agreements that followed.

This history makes clear that the attitude adopted by the IMF towards the disbursal of its own funds can affect debtor-creditor negotiations. The change in IMF policy in 1987–8, which allowed multilateral funds to begin flowing again, together with policy reform, promoted the resumption of private-sector funding.

4   Options for reform

We now consider options for reforming the procedures for dealing with sovereign debt crises. A number of these schemes, it turns out, are non-starters. But the purpose of this section is to provide an analysis and critique of the various proposals. Readers interested only in our own agenda for reform can go directly to section 5.

4.1   Bondholders' protective committees

In the wake of the Mexican crisis Macmillan (1995) and others have suggested that representative committees should be resuscitated: that they could again provide a solution to the renegotiation problem. As in the nineteenth century and the 1930s, bondholders would appoint representatives to negotiate with a government in financial difficulty and restructure its debts. The steering committee might include representatives of emerging market mutual funds, pension funds, banks, large individual investors and perhaps a representative of creditor-country governments (see section 5).

That this approach has some relevance today is suggested by the fact that uninsured trade creditors, a very disparate group of investors, have formed representative committees in an effort to recover their money from various former Soviet republics.[18] Countries would still have to impose a unilateral stay for a limited period to halt the investors' rush for the exits. But the question of with whom to negotiate would have a less confusing answer.

This is not to say that all confusion would evaporate. In the era of bond finance, as described above, there typically existed a host of competing committees. Sometimes several competing committees would claim responsibility for negotiating over a particular defaulted bond issue or with a particular government. As different bondholders signed up with different committees, it became difficult for any one spokesperson to represent their views credibly, and governments found it difficult to conduct coherent negotiations. In the United States, where such confusion was particularly severe in the early 1930s, the US State Department ameliorated it by lending its seal of approval to the Foreign Bondholders Protective Council, which then became the dominant bondholders' representative organ. It might similarly make sense for creditor-country governments and the IMF to recognize one or more committees to speak for the bondholders. (It would not be necessary to adopt legislation giving formal prerogatives to such a committee. G–7 governments and the IMF would simply say that they were prepared to work with a particular committee.) This would have the merit of allowing the bondholders' committee to evolve as an informal organization of creditors akin to the Paris and London Clubs. If the committee in question failed to provide effective representation to the bondholders, nothing would prevent competitors from springing up. Official recognition of a particular committee would only prevent entry not motivated by significant inefficiency.

Even when the Council of Foreign Bondholders enjoyed comparable prerogatives, however, many years could still be required to conclude an agreement. In the absence of full information about the strength of the government and the resolve of the bondholders, the two engaged in an extended war of attrition, each withholding concessions and attempting to wear down the opponent. The ability of the Council of Foreign Bondholders to bargain effectively was enhanced by its close working relationship with the London Stock Exchange, which prevented countries from floating new issues prior to settlement and even barred organized trading in defaulted debts. Now that there are organized stock markets in many financial centres such arrangements would be more difficult to enforce. It is not clear that bondholders' representative committees would possess the leverage needed to compel a quick conclusion to negotiations. If they proved as effective as they were in the nineteenth century and the 1930s, many months or years might still be required to complete a negotiated settlement. That uninsured trade creditors who formed a committee to get their money out of Russia and other former Soviet republics have little to show for their efforts after three years is not particularly encouraging.

A model clause in debt instruments (see below) could provide for a restructuring package to be negotiated by a particular bondholders' committee on behalf of all bondholders, with recourse to arbitration for dissenting creditors. This would remove uncertainty about which assets fell under the domain of the committee. But giving seniority to new money would probably not be acceptable *ex ante*; it would have to depend on agreement of bondholders case-by-case, with the incentive that this could restore the debtor's liquidity.

The arguments above suggest that there may be a need to complement bondholders' committees with other institutional changes of the sort we now consider.

4.2 New contractual arrangements to enhance *ex-ante* efficiency

The purpose of reforming procedures to restructure sovereign debt is to enhance the efficiency of the lending process. This can be approached by improving contractual loan agreements at inception as well as by reforming the reorganization post-default. One approach to *ex-ante* reform is to alter contractual arrangements for sovereign financing. It turns out, unfortunately, that there are serious problems with using contractual arrangements to carry out this role. An important impediment is the lack of clarity of lenders' property rights in the event of default and an unwillingness on the part of some sovereign states to permit the enforcement of claims. Legislation in member states of the EU has clarified the extent of any immunity in commercial transactions and the process of enforcement; this is an example which could be imitated.

4.2.1 Defining property rights and their enforcement

In contrast to the position of a private company where all its assets will usually be available to creditors, for several reasons only a very small proportion of a state's assets will be available for execution. Most of the country's assets will be located in its own territory and may therefore be beyond the reach of any court or tribunal. Exports can be transferred to private (third-country) owners before they leave the debtor state's borders. Foreign courts will only allow the creditor's rights to be enforced against the debtor if property rights are clearly defined in the debtor's jurisdiction. While the debtor state may have some assets within the jurisdiction of the courts in another country, it is frequently very difficult to levy execution against such assets, because of the law of sovereign immunity. Although most states no longer accord sovereign immunity from suit in an action in respect of a loan transaction or other debt instrument, states still enjoy a wide immunity from execution against their property. Unless the state has waived that immunity or the property is clearly in use for commercial purposes, execution or prejudgment attachment will not be available in most jurisdictions.

The United States Foreign Sovereign Immunities Act, Section 1610(a)(2), goes further and precludes execution even against commercial property unless it has a connection with the subject matter of the action against the foreign state (a requirement which also features in a draft convention produced by the International Law Commission). Embassy bank accounts in most states and the treatment of central bank accounts varies (though in the United Kingdom such accounts enjoy absolute immunity). Even if immunity has been waived in respect of state property, property in the hands of separate legal entities will not be liable to execution in respect of obligations entered into by the state unless the forum state can be persuaded to lift the corporate veil.

4.2.2 Improved collateralization

Providing collateral would directly strengthen the bonding function of the loan contract or bond covenant. But in the case of sovereign debt, the provision of collateral is problematic. This is evident in the historical experience of secured creditors, who supposedly enjoy the benefits of collateral. In the inter-war period creditors experienced significant problems when attempting to secure greater payouts on secured debt compared with unsecured debt. The rationale was that if the creditor could not get possession of the assets, it did not deserve a greater payout than unsecured creditors. The Polish 'copper loans' of 1977, supposedly secured on export earnings, did not obtain favourable treatment in Polish debt restructuring.

One frequently mentioned possibility is to attach assets outside the debtor's border or to apply liens to exports. The courts of some countries have been prepared to authorize such measures. But enforcement is very difficult. If a country successfully managed to export the asset, is there adequate provision in international law for law suits to succeed in third party countries, for example? Could a creditor obtain possession of oil transported by Nigeria to France using French courts if its loan were secured on Nigerian oil?

None of this is to deny that it would be efficiency-enhancing to clarify the legal status of liens against sovereign governments and private companies. But even if a loan were repayable from specific sources of income such as the revenue of the national petroleum company, as with the US loan to Mexico in 1995, there remains the question of enforcement. In this case, the arrangement requires Mexico to honour its contractual obligations with the United States and continue to pump oil; if it does not, there is no assurance of repayment. More generally, if property rights in the creditor country are not well defined or if enforcement is weak or costly, collateral will have a lower value. Legal and contractual changes that facilitate enforcement and thereby improve the debt contract will allow not only lower interest rates, but also a greater variety of debt contracts.

4.2.3 The development of new financial instruments to enhance risk sharing

If a country's main source of income comes from exploiting a single asset such as a mineral reserve whose price is highly volatile, its capital structure should reflect this. It would seem foolish to borrow. Indeed, it would probably be almost as unwise for the country to finance all costs of production with its own equity. The obvious route would be a risk-sharing arrangement whereby another country or corporation took a large slice of the risk in return for part of the revenue.

In practice, however, the markets for such financial instruments have proven difficult to develop. The International Finance Corporation has offered put options to investors to enable them to limit their downside risk on individual projects; the market in these options did not take off. Commodity bonds have been widely proposed, but no instrument that has been developed has gained wide currency. It would be helpful to promote the creation and widening of these markets.

4.2.4 Limits on the government's capital structure to prevent risk hoarding

While the development of certain kinds of new financial assets can encourage risk sharing, others can lead to an undue concentration of sovereign risk. Mexico's experience suggests that certain capital structures are particularly susceptible to destabilizing shocks. The fact that the Mexican government's tesobonos were dollar-linked (interest paid was effectively indexed to the dollar) meant that a shock which required devaluation could be especially destabilizing.[19] Similarly, one of the conditions that may lead to a self-fulfilling debt run is large quantities of short-term debt (Giavazzi and Pagano, 1990). Denominating short-term debt in foreign currency compounds the vulnerability.

Theory suggests a country will get better terms in the market if it can precommit to restrict the maturity structure, currency denomination or level of its debt, for example, by adopting a statute or constitutional amendment committing it not to exceed a maximum ratio of debt (foreign or total) to GNP, as in the Maastricht Treaty. In practice, however, there are questions about the effectiveness of self-imposed debt limitations (von Hagen, 1991); parliaments that adopt them can also revoke them, after all. And such restrictions may also have significant costs in terms of forgone fiscal flexibility. In any case, while fiscal restrictions may provide investors with some protection against over-borrowing, they do not address debt-servicing problems that arise because of, say, commodity-price or interest-rate shocks.

4.2.5 Dispersal of debt to parastatals and privatization

When all external debt takes the form of claims on the central government or implicit government guarantees apply, default becomes an all-or-nothing proposition and can threaten the stability of the country's financial system. Dispersal of debt without implicit or explicit guarantees would provide diversification of managerial failure.[20] It enforces financial discipline on the local governments and quasi-public enterprises that incur the obligations. This is not 'fronting' sovereign government borrowing through public enterprises but rather bringing market discipline into borrowing that would otherwise come under central government.

Relating debt to the revenue and managerial activities of particular quasi-public enterprises without central government guarantee would also reduce systemic risk. If debt is an obligation of a railway or petroleum company rather than the central government and the authorities can credibly commit not to bail out the company in the event that it experiences financial difficulties, these difficulties have no necessary implications for the public finances. In so far as the revenue of, say, the petroleum company depends on oil prices on world markets rather than domestic economic conditions, its correlation with the revenue of other quasi-public enterprises – and with the tax revenue of the government – will be imperfect, providing some protection through diversification against macroeconomic shocks.

These are measures that the borrowers and lenders can adopt in so far as they regard them as desirable. But the devolution of borrowing can only be accomplished where debt can be collateralized by assets that can service it, as in the case of trading or industrial companies owned by the state or entities with tax-raising powers.[21] The fact that some two-thirds of all long-term private capital flows to developing countries go to nominally private entities suggests that there is scope for pursuing this strategy. Privatization itself is a limiting case of devolving debts and diversifying managerial failure, and one objective of privatization is precisely to permit an enterprise to fail if that is economically justified.

None of this ensures that the government will necessarily be able to resist pressure to assume responsibility for the debts of private enterprises like banks and quasi-public enterprises such as transport and utility companies. Imagine a strategic game between the quasi-public enterprise and the central government, in which the former delays agreeing to a restructuring in the hope that the latter will ride to its rescue to avoid the negative repercussions on its own creditworthiness, the result of which would be additional delay in reaching a settlement.[22] In addition, multiplying the number of distinct debtors in the borrowing country may increase renegotiation costs, especially when many defaults occur at once. Another disadvantage of this approach is that a refusal to provide guarantees may increase the cost of debt. Since the debt of one activity will not co-insure another, the higher interest rate will reflect the greater risk assumed by the lender. But the objection that governments will be forced to 'nationalize' the debts, as happened frequently in the 1980s, ignores the change since in attitudes towards privatization and towards letting large firms (including banks) fail.

Thus each of these proposals has significant limitations, but there are elements of each that we shall be able to use.

4.3 Providing *ex ante* for *ex-post* procedures

A further step in modifying contractual terms would be to recognize the possibility of renegotiation explicitly in debt instruments. There is no reason why a sovereign loan agreement could not provide that a stated majority of creditors could agree to alter its financial terms in the event of default. This would attenuate the free-rider problem addressed by provisions for 'cramdown' in corporate bankruptcy codes.

Debt agreements regularly cede prerogatives – such as the right to accelerate payment – to majority rule. To prevent creditors from rushing to court and forestalling the imposition of a restructuring package, the debt instrument could specify that no enforcement of its provisions would be possible for a certain period following a default. Bond covenants could also make provision for recourse to an arbitral tribunal for creditors dissatisfied by the terms of settlement (because, for example, the rescheduling goes beyond what is permitted by the terms of the loan contract).

International discussions might be directed towards formulating 'model clauses' that could be incorporated into sovereign debt instruments. Following Greenwood and Mercer (1995), model clauses might include provisions like the following:

- The obligations of a sovereign debtor could be reduced if a restructuring package was agreed by a specified majority of creditors.

- A restructuring package amending the obligations of a sovereign debtor would also have to be approved by the IMF or some other institution.

- In the event of default (suspension of debt service), no action could be taken by creditors for a specified period, pending completion of arbitration procedures (described in more detail below).

- Claims by creditors who objected to the restructuring agreed on their behalf by a bondholders' committee, ratified by a majority of bondholders and approved by the IMF, would be referred to a dedicated arbitral tribunal (again, see below). The loan agreement or bond covenant would provide for such recourse to ensure that national courts regarded its findings as binding and thereby to avoid the delay, uncertainty and cost of legal proceedings.

- Failure of the debtor state to incorporate similar clauses in future loan agreements would constitute an act of default.

There seems no reason why agreements for syndicated (bank) loans to sovereigns should not include such provisions as well. Greenwood and Mercer's scheme is intended to provide a comprehensive approach to debt restructuring, which includes having recourse to a dedicated arbitral tribunal. Note, however, that it would be possible in principle to implement the first, third and fifth of these clauses without provision for an arbitral tribunal.

Unlike bankruptcy procedures that interfere with the normal functioning of contracts, this approach is based on mutual consent of private lenders and sovereign borrowers in recognition of the gain in *ex-post* efficiency it could yield. The magnitude of spreads on bank loans to sovereign borrowers and on the bond issues of governments and quasi-public enterprises clearly indicates the existence of a significant perceived probability of capital loss owing to default. Yet there are no recognized procedures for dealing with that contingency when it arises, as it inevitably does (for otherwise the lending would be risk free, at the risk-free rate). Procedures that reduce *ex ante* the uncertainty of how default will be resolved, providing orderly as opposed to disorderly workouts, will improve the *ex-ante* position of lenders and therefore the market terms. As we pointed out at the beginning of section 2, debt contracts without such provisions are exceptional. With the increasing globalization of markets, it is perhaps more important now than before that sovereign debt contracts should no longer be exceptional in this regard.

It might be argued that investors would not be prepared to accept measures which enhanced the efficiency of the settlement process *ex post* at the expense of weakening the *ex-ante* bonding role of debt. If so, they would be inclined to restrict the supply and raise the cost of credit to sovereign borrowers.[23] This objection is subject to two important qualifications. First, the reduction of the risk premium from making provision for orderly workouts and minimizing uncertainty may dominate any increase in the risk premium owing to any perceived weakening of the *ex-ante* bonding role of debt. Second, it would be possible, as we suggest in section 5 below, to supplement orderly workouts with other measures that would strengthen the incentive to adhere to the *ex-ante* terms of loan contracts.

4.4   Closing the courts to creditors through statute or treaty

Another proposal is for countries to close their courts to 'rogue' creditors seeking to challenge a restructuring endorsed by an overwhelming majority (Hurlock, 1995). The rationale again is to facilitate restructuring by preventing a small minority of creditors from holding up a negotiated settlement. An amendment to the US Foreign Sovereign Immunities Act, for example, could extend immunity from suit to a foreign state in respect of a loan transaction forming part of its external debt and protect its property from attachment if a majority of similarly situated creditors (or the IMF) had endorsed a restructuring.

Implementation of this proposal faces serious obstacles. For example, all of the major creditor countries would have to adopt the appropriate changes in statute to produce the desired effect. A country adopting such a statute could attempt to convince other states that international comity required them to refuse to enforce a debt agreement on behalf of a small minority of creditors. But judicial reactions to arguments based on comity vary across jurisdictions. Judges in different countries might interpret the provisions differently. Some national courts might prevent creditors from enforcing claims against a debtor state and grant seniority for new money to a country which had restructured its debt, while others might not.[24]

In principle, this problem could be solved through the negotiation of an international treaty between creditor and debtor states, which would then give effect to the treaty in their national laws. In practice, however, this seems unlikely. As Greenwood and Mercer (1995) note, the trend in recent years has been away from sovereign immunity. In addition, closing the courts to creditors through the negotiation of an international treaty might be deemed to contravene Article 6 of the European Convention of Human Rights, Paragraph 1 of which states: 'In the determination of his civil rights and obligations ... everyone is entitled to a fair and public hearing within a reasonable time by an independent and impartial tribunal established by law'. This would certainly not apply, however, if creditors had voluntarily accepted arbitration *ex ante*, as suggested in section 4.3 above.

4.5 Coordinating a temporary standstill through IMF Article VIII(2)(b)

The difficulty of negotiating an international treaty provides the rationale for foreclosing the litigation option through reinterpretation or amendment of the IMF's Articles of Agreement. Article VIII(2)(b) provides that 'exchange contracts which involve the currency of any member and which are contrary to the exchange control regulations of that member maintained or imposed consistently with this Agreement shall be unenforceable in the territories of any member'. If a government were to suspend repayment of its debt with the approval of the IMF, a debt contract which required payment in foreign currency might be rendered unenforceable in the courts of any IMF member state under the terms of Article VIII(2)(b).

This assumes that the term 'exchange contract' can be interpreted sufficiently broadly to include not just the imposition of exchange controls but also a standstill or stay on state debt. This does not appear to have been the original intent of the clause, nor has it been the interpretation of the courts of the United States and United Kingdom (the courts of France have subscribed to a more liberal interpretation). In any case, in the United States and the United Kingdom, according to Mann (1992), Article VIII(2)(b) has been interpreted as being concerned with the initial legality of a contract rather than with its subsequent enforceability.

The IMF Executive Board could give Article VIII(2)(b) a new, definitive interpretation broadening its coverage. This would have to make clear that the article applies to defaults as such, not just to the imposition of exchange controls. The question is whether mere reinterpretation would have sufficient force. If such a reinterpretation were not deemed to have legal effect, Article VIII(2)(b) could be formally amended to make clear its applicability to defaults as well as exchange controls and explicitly to exclude legal recourse by dissident creditors.

Amending the IMF Articles of Agreement is difficult in practice. It requires approval by 50% of the member countries, with 85% of the total voting power (determined for each member by its quota). In any case it would remain for the national courts to accept the Articles' new provisions or interpretation. Most member states would need to introduce legislation to put the provisions of such an amendment (overriding domestic contract law) into effect domestically. Politically, this is a problem: imagine the resistance in the national parliaments and congresses of the major creditor countries to legislation that would limit the rights of their investors overseas.

It might also be objected that exchange controls are ineffective, distortionary and costly. But it is hard to see how a stay could be enforced otherwise. There is ample evidence that temporary capital controls are indeed effective (Eichengreen, Rose and Wyplosz, 1994; Marston, 1993; Obstfeld, 1993). The distortionary costs of such temporary measures would be dwarfed by even a small reduction in the harshness of macroeconomic restrictions that might be imposed by the unconstrained markets.

4.6   An international bankruptcy court or tribunal

None of the measures enumerated above would empower an international court or multilateral institution to play a supervisory role comparable with that exercised by a national court in bankruptcy proceedings.[25] Supervising the negotiation of a reorganization plan would not be within the power of the International Court of Justice, for example, which has jurisdiction only over cases between states, not between a state and private parties (such as private foreign creditors). This has led to proposals (for example Sachs, 1995; Greenwood and Mercer, 1995) for the creation of an international arbitral tribunal with jurisdiction over debt disputes between states or between states and private creditors, possibly as an agency of the International Monetary Fund.

Creation of the tribunal, funding for its operations and binding status for its determinations could be provided by an international treaty or by an amendment to the IMF Articles of Agreement. Alternatively, the tribunal could be a self-standing entity independent of the Fund, possibly relying on staff support from it or another multilateral institution. There are two issues here. One is whether implementation is feasible: whether such a tribunal could override national laws, whether it could act in binding arbitration, or whether it would be limited to coordination, conciliation and advice. The other issue is the role to be played by the IMF. We consider the first question in this section and the second one in section 4.8.

Precedent for an arbitral tribunal with jurisdiction over cases between states or between states and private creditors can be found in, *inter alia*, the Iran-United States Tribunal, which has heard cases brought by official and private claimants. A government could petition the tribunal to initiate a proceeding, much as Chapter 9 of the US code permits a municipality to petition the courts for reorganization in bankruptcy. Possibly creditor-country governments or the managing director of the IMF could also have the right to initiate proceedings. The relevant decision-making body would then decide whether the petition had merit, and if so authorize the government to impose a unilateral suspension so as to prevent the creditors from rushing for the exits.[26]

The tribunal would then help creditors and the debtor to negotiate a debt restructuring. Were the IMF given this role, it would proceed under authority vested in it by Article V(2)(b), which empowers the IMF to perform financial and technical services if authorized to do so by its members. The process would involve examining the economic and financial situation of the country, the stance of policy and the state of the international financial markets. The relevant officials would consult with representatives of the creditors, perhaps encouraging the establishment of a creditors' representative committee. The plan would entail reorganization of the debt and policy adjustments by the debtor government. It would come into operation if approved by the debtor government and a majority (perhaps qualified) of creditors. The facility or tribunal could have the power to cram down generally agreed settlement terms. The plan might entail agreement by the creditors to provide new money, although this would be difficult to enforce where the government's liabilities take the form of bonded debt. This provides a rationale for empowering the facility to grant seniority to new funds and/or inject new money of its own.

There are several distinctions that might delineate the scope of such a tribunal: type of debt instrument (bond or bank loan); residence of lender; 'proper law' of the debt contract; currency of denomination of the debt (domestic or foreign). A key question is whether limits on recourse and the decisions of the tribunal should apply to domestic as well as foreign creditors. Many of the inefficiencies that these institutions are designed to avert can arise equally from the actions of domestic and foreign residents. Both can and do hold the foreign-currency liabilities of governments, and the actions of both classes of creditors have the capacity to provoke a run on official reserves. In the recent Mexican crisis, for example, much of the flight from government debt appears to have been on the part of Mexican residents.[27] Any attempt to extend differential treatment to domestic and foreign creditors would open the door to all manner of circumvention, with one group employing the other as its surrogate.

To produce an effective standstill and impose an effective reorganization plan, the jurisdiction of the tribunal might therefore have to apply equally to domestic and foreign investors. Which government liabilities would fall under the jurisdiction of the tribunal would be for the government and its creditors to decide when specifying the terms of the loan agreement; a government could always exclude such clauses from the contracts underlying its domestic currency liabilities. If the right of recourse of dissident creditors to the tribunal were specified in the original bond covenant, as described above, this would not pose obvious problems.

How would the activities of such a tribunal differ from existing IMF procedures for dealing with countries in financial distress? First, allowing the tribunal to invoke the standstill would deal with the 'verification problem' and thereby mitigate the damage to the country's reputation of the suspension of debt service payments. Reputation will be preserved only if the markets believe that financial distress was not the debtor's 'fault'; but then the contingency responsible for the crisis must be independently verifiable. The theory of 'escape clauses' suggests that measures of this sort can be invoked without damage to a government's reputation only when the contingency in response to which they are utilized is independently verifiable. The difficulty of verification explains why governments have been reluctant to employ unilateral suspensions in practice.

To the extent that the problem was judged to be the debtor's fault, of course, a standstill might still be justifiable, but then the debtor's reputation *should* suffer. Independent endorsement of a standstill could also limit contagion to other countries and other assets, in so far as the tribunal could point out the specific circumstances that warranted suspension of service on a class of obligations of a given debtor. The moral hazard – the 'strategic' use of a standstill to pressure creditors – would be limited by the possibility that it would not be approved.

Under the tribunal proposal, this body would assume the role of 'referee' more directly than the IMF does currently. Binding status for its determinations would eliminate the problem of 'holdout' by a minority of creditors. An ability to assign seniority to new funds would diminish problems of illiquidity. Alternatively, a tribunal which worked in concert with the IMF could ameliorate the problem of injecting new money directly.

To limit moral hazard and improve *ex-ante* efficiency might require strengthening the powers of the IMF, by allowing it to impose stronger policy conditionality on governments in return for allowing them to make use of the binding arbitration powers of the tribunal. It might be provided that only countries which had met IMF conditionality *ex ante* could have recourse to this binding arbitration *ex post*. This assumes that the IMF would be able to avoid the obvious time inconsistency problem. Though it would be in its interest to announce that binding arbitration would be extended only to countries that had met its conditionality, after the fact it might have every incentive to make an exception, which would weaken the incentive for countries to satisfy its conditions in the first place.

The tribunal would not possess the powers of a national court to enforce seizure of collateral, given sovereign immunity. Granting seniority to new money would require a treaty agreed between debtor and creditor nations which would then have to be implemented in national law. (Alternatively, this could be provided for by agreement in advance as part of the loan agreement or bond covenant, as described in section 4.2 above.) Creating an arbitral tribunal with the power to require dissident creditors to accept a majority-approved restructuring would require an international treaty.

Whether the debtors and creditors would support such an initiative is uncertain. To secure the support of debtor governments it would be necessary to reassure them that their sovereignty would not be compromised. It would be desirable therefore to include in any agreement establishing a tribunal provisions analogous to those of Chapter 9, which state that the court may not interfere with the government's political or economic powers.

Securing the support of creditor-country governments would not be straightforward either. The industrial countries might be reluctant to participate if doing so raised the possibility that they too might be forced to surrender significant independence. In principle, there is no reason why such procedures should be limited to developing countries. Given the amounts of money involved, it can be argued that it is potentially more important for the international community to consider ways of providing 'orderly workouts' in the developed world. But it is not clear that the governments of high-income countries would see a need to subject themselves to the authority of the tribunal. Allowing some countries to announce that they were prepared to participate only as creditors, however, would threaten to label the others as second-class citizens in the eyes of the capital markets. Provisions analogous to those of Chapter 9 which allow only municipal governments and not their creditors to petition the court would reassure the industrial countries that the tribunal would consider their debt management policies only at their own volition, but they still might balk.[28]

To recapitulate, there are significant obstacles to the establishment of a 'bankruptcy court' and procedure modelled on Chapter 11. We judge them to be insurmountable for the foreseeable future. In particular, because of the great divergences that exist among national perspectives and laws on the best ways of dealing with problems of bankruptcy, it is unlikely that countries will be able to agree on a treaty or amendment to IMF Articles and implement its provisions in national legislation, as necessary to give legal effect to such an institution.

There are strong arguments, however, behind some of the functions that such an institution and procedure would fulfil. We discuss below how elements at least might be implemented by alternative means.

4.7   A mediation and conciliation service

A more modest option on related lines may still be feasible. It would be possible to create an independent agency that would act, on a voluntary basis and by mutual consent, as coordinator, conciliator and arbitrator. As we explain in section 4.8, it is also conceivable that the agency in question could be both independent and affiliated with, say, the IMF. Determining its functions precisely still requires answers to some of the difficult questions posed above, but it might be possible to create an effective agency of this kind without a treaty or national legislation (although the analogous ICSID – see below – was established by a treaty).

Such an agency could carry out a number of distinct functions. It could sanction a temporary standstill in payments when (advised by the IMF) it judged this action on the part of the debtor government to be necessary; while its endorsement would have no legal force, it would limit contagion and the negative effects on the debtor's reputation, as above. It could provide mediation and conciliation services in negotiations between the debtor and creditors and, if desired by the parties themselves, binding arbitration. It could provide a source of appeal for a minority of investors dissatisfied by the terms of settlement, arbitrating disputes among different classes of creditors, as in the Greenwood-Mercer proposal. In some respects the functions and structure of this agency would resemble those of the International Center for the Settlement of Investment Disputes (ICSID) or the UK Advisory Conciliation and Arbitration Service (ACAS) in labour-management negotiations. That is, it would act as a forum, a referee, an adviser and sometimes a true arbiter. The ICSID provides conciliation and arbitration facilities for disputes between governments and foreign private enterprises. Many countries have bilateral agreements committing themselves to accept ICSID decisions, and such recourse can also be written into individual contracts.

A further potential role of this agency would be to coordinate negotiations between the Paris Club, the London Club and the bondholders' committee(s). There is already some coordination between the London and Paris Clubs.[29] Currently, this mostly occurs *de facto* through the Paris Club's taking the lead and demanding 'comparable treatment' of other creditors. But the comparable-treatment provision has no legal force, and its effectiveness remains to be studied. In any case, the problem will grow more complicated with the addition of a third ring to the circus, and there are also creditors which would not be included in any of the three rings (creditor governments outside the Paris Club, uninsured trade creditors, etc.). The agency would also be in contact with them.

4.8   Roles for the IMF

As the previous discussion suggests, the IMF will surely have a major role in any new procedure for orderly workouts. The question is how major. There are arguments both for and against concentrating power and responsibility in the hands of the Fund. The argument for is based on considerations of speed and information. The IMF already possesses an Executive Board and economists with specialized skills who can evaluate a country's policies and financing needs and judge whether its stay of payments is justified. Indeed, the Fund has long played the first of these roles in Paris Club negotiations, and its certification of 'imminent default' in that context is not far from the second. The IMF, through the operation of its Capital Markets Division and country missions, is privy to the most up-to-date information on economic conditions available outside the government (see Calvo and Goldstein, 1995). By sharing the facts, it can overcome the informational asymmetries that lend negotiations between debtors and creditors their war-of-attrition character and block quick settlement. If other functions were also assigned to the Fund, it would be straightforward to coordinate the different parts of the workout procedure. Considerations of efficiency and speed argue for concentrating these functions under one roof.

The argument against is based on potential conflict of interest. Under domestic law, debt adjustment is overseen by independent judicial officials. This independence would not necessarily carry over to the Executive Board of the IMF, which is in some respects a political body that may not be well-suited to exercising quasi-judicial functions, even indirectly. The countries affected by its decisions are, after all, also the shareholders of the IMF. Further, there might be significant incentive incompatibilities among some subset of the Fund's activities, including:

- Acting as *ex-ante* policy adviser to a debtor whose policies may subsequently be judged to have 'failed' (whose fault? is that relevant to eligibility for debt restructuring?).

- Being a priority creditor.

- Being the major source of information to other lenders.

- Acting as negotiator and/or arbiter of a debt restructuring that might impose writedowns on dissident creditors.

- Acting as the authority imposing conditionality on the debtor.

- Serving as the source of new lending.

This argues for establishing any entity that carries out signalling, mediation and conciliation, or arbitration functions (with or without binding powers) as a self-standing body separate from the Executive Board – indeed, separate from the IMF. Separate provision could be made for the representation of private creditors, since they would not be members of a public international organization. Staff support could be provided by the Bank for International Settlements (BIS), or if that were thought outside the BIS's normal remit, or the BIS were viewed as too much a 'rich man's club' to be impartial, then by an independent secretariat.

Alternatively, the IMF could establish an affiliated but independent institution, analogous to the International Centre for Settlement of Investment Disputes of the World Bank.

Were these functions to be carried out by an independent entity, what roles would the IMF then assume? It could advise on the justification (or absence of justification) for a standstill; it could provide information to all parties (the Paris Club, the London Club, the bondholders' committee(s), the independent agency and the debtor); and it could provide new money, where necessary, subject to strict policy conditionality.

Evidently the Fund could go beyond advising the debtor country and a tribunal or another agency on the advisability of a standstill and could itself issue an opinion on whether the country's unilateral suspension is justified. A definitive reinterpretation of Article VIII(2)(b) would support the IMF in this role even if it did not have legal effect in national courts. Ideally, however, nations would give effect to this provision in national law. Otherwise, Executive Directors might find it difficult to endorse a standstill which could be regarded as a breach of contract in their countries' courts.

There are valid objections to the idea that governments in positions like Mexico's in 1994–5 should be encouraged to contemplate the suspension of debt service payments and that the IMF should provide sanction for its actions where it regarded them to be justified. For example, a standstill on certain assets might encourage exit from non-stayed assets. A country suspending debt service might therefore be inclined to buttress this step with the application of exchange controls. The more integrated a country has become into the international financial system, the more comprehensive and onerous these controls would have to be in order to be effective. Controls are costly to remove as well as to impose; there is the danger that their application could create a constituency for their retention. A payments stay might also provoke exit by investors from the assets of other countries.

The question is not whether problems exist, however – surely they do – but whether they are likely to be more or less severe if other approaches were adopted. A large loan from creditor-country governments and the IMF, as in the case of Mexico, would probably do less to provoke exit from non-stayed assets in both the country experiencing the crisis and other countries. But creditor governments and the Fund either lack the resources necessary to extend loans of the same magnitude in the future or are not prepared to do so for political reasons or for fear of moral hazard. In any case, as we argue below, new money is not always the appropriate response to a Mexico-style problem. Drastic monetary and fiscal retrenchment might succeed in reassuring investors, entirely obviating the need for a stay, but at very high cost to the domestic economy. Indeed, if the cost were massive unemployment that eroded political support for the government, the policy might not be sustainable and would even fail to reassure the markets. A payments stay creates problems that justify concern, but there may be circumstances under which there is no preferable alternative.

4.9   Recapitulation

While there exist appealing arguments for the reform proposals enumerated above, most have significant drawbacks, which we summarize here:

- *Bondholders' committees.* Their creation would not halt the creditors' rush for the exits. Countries that have been reluctant to suspend debt service payments unilaterally for fear of damaging their reputations would have no incentive to behave differently. Settlement would still take time, and the injection of new money would remain difficult.

- *Contractual innovations.* Measures designed to strengthen collateralization are unlikely to be enforceable. Assigning responsibility for debts to quasi-public enterprises rather than the central government is no guarantee against a bailout. Self-imposed debt limits place the fiscal authorities in a macroeconomic straitjacket and are unlikely to be credible.

- *Closing the courts to creditors through statute or treaty.* Preventing a small band of dissident creditors from using legal means to hold up a restructuring would not address the other problems with current procedures. In any case, there is likely to be significant resistance in the creditor countries to measures which weaken bondholders' prerogatives.

- *Coordinating reform through IMF Article VIII(2)(b).* This proposal is subject to the same objections raised by the idea of closing the courts.

- *An international bankruptcy court.* An international court or tribunal with powers analogous to those enjoyed by bankruptcy courts in the United States is a non-starter given the very great legal obstacles to implementation. Were such obstacles to be surmounted, the desirability of such a procedure would still remain unclear. Even operating under a treaty, such an international court would be unlikely to possess the powers of a national court to enforce seizure of collateral, given sovereign immunity. It would not be able to replace the government of a country the way bankruptcy courts replace the management of firms. The danger of moral hazard would be great.

- *A mediation and arbitration service.* An agency to mediate negotiations between debtors and creditors might speed the process of settlement, but it is not clear that an independent agency would have the superior access to information necessary to overcome informational asymmetries. Nor would it obviously solve other problems like obstacles to the provision of new money.

- *An expanded role for the IMF.* Without giving it binding powers of enforcement analogous to those enjoyed by national bankruptcy courts, it would be possible to empower the IMF to undertake similar functions on a more modest scale: granting or withholding endorsement of a country's stay of payments; mediating and conciliating between creditors and the debtor; coordinating the deliberations of the Paris Club, the London Club and the bondholders' committee(s). But the Fund is not independent of political influence from governments that are interested parties in negotiations; and there might be significant incentive incompatibilities among its various activities.

5   An agenda for reform

Notwithstanding these drawbacks, each of these proposals has desirable features. In this section we therefore offer a proposal for reform which combines elements of the alternative approaches.

As will become apparent, it would be possible to adopt some of these recommendations without also embracing others. But there are important complementarities among the reforms we propose. They would do most to enhance the efficiency of the debt restructuring process if implemented as a package.

5.1   Recommendations

5.1.1   The creation of bondholders' committees

Creating bondholders' representative committees would minimize uncertainty about the locus of authority in negotiations. History suggests that a confusing proliferation of committees can spring up in the absence of official accreditation. This danger increases with the globalization of markets. It may be desirable therefore for the governments of the major creditor countries (or the G–7, the G–10, or the Interim Committee) to recognize a single international committee ('The Bondholders Council') as the representative of the bondholders. But a single committee could be overly powerful and even obstructive. Competition between the CFB and the FBPC in the 1930s and 1940s encouraged each to show flexibility. Hence some counterbalance might be needed (for example, one or more representatives from governments or multilateral institutions on the steering committee of the Council). There is no case, however, for separate committees to deal with different classes of bondholders – one purpose of the Bondholders Council is precisely to resolve conflicts among classes of bondholders.

While we need not be too specific here about the constitution and operations of the Bondholders Council, it is clear that it will be less collegial, with less repeated interaction, than the Paris Club. But speedy negotiation will be essential. This argues for a charter, a permanent secretariat, at least a minimal set of conventions and a core of permanent members (supplemented by members with major positions in the case at hand). Note that in practice, the market 'shakeout' during a crisis would be likely to lead to a more concentrated distribution of securities *ex post* than there had been *ex ante*, and this would facilitate negotiation in the Bondholders Council; in that respect, the thickness and liquidity of today's markets are an advantage in comparison with the 1930s, when trading after 1931 was sparse.

While the Bondholders Council would be responsible for restructuring bonded debts, the London and Paris Clubs would retain their responsibility for bank loans and official credits. It would be important, therefore, to coordinate deliberations in the three venues. This could be done tacitly. The Paris Club could go first, making agreement to a restructuring contingent on the government's prior agreement with the IMF. The Bondholders Council and the London Club would follow.

5.1.2   A mediation and conciliation service

Negotiations between the debtor and the Bondholders Council are likely to remain distressingly slow relative to the lightning-quick response of international markets.

They should therefore be aided by the creation of a mediation service for conciliation and voluntary arbitration. Because a major purpose of such a service is to overcome resistance to settlement created by informational asymmetries, it would be important for such an agency to be privy to up-to-date information, which argues for IMF involvement. The agency might also take on other functions, as we discussed above (for example, dealing with the other creditor representative groups, helping to coordinate negotiations, or endorsing a payments standstill).

5.1.3   Contractual innovations

Changes in bond covenants to permit a majority of creditors to alter the terms of payment would further speed settlement. This would prevent a small minority of dissident creditors from holding up negotiations. Lenders' property rights should be clarified, so as to give lenders greater confidence that legal remedies are available to the creditor in the event of sovereign default. Reducing this uncertainty will reduce interest rates and allow a wider variety of contracts in sovereign lending, which in turn will improve risk sharing between borrowers and lenders.

5.1.4   An arbitral tribunal

To make the aforementioned changes in the provisions of loan contracts palatable to potential lenders, dissident creditors would have recourse to an arbitral tribunal. This might or might not be subsumed in the mediation and conciliation agency. Loan agreements would specify that minority creditors could appeal to the tribunal to block a negotiated agreement, and with that contractual protection, the tribunal's findings could not be disputed in court.[30] To prevent the IMF from being saddled with too many different, potentially conflicting responsibilities, there is an argument for establishing the tribunal as an affiliated but independent institution, perhaps analogous to the International Centre for Settlement of Investment Disputes of the World Bank.

5.1.5   New roles for the IMF

Governments have the capacity to impose the equivalent of creditor standstills by suspending debt service payments and/or temporarily imposing exchange controls. But they hesitate to do so for fear that they will jeopardize their future credit market access. Encouraging the IMF to advise the debtor or another agency on the justification (or not) for a suspension of debt service payments would allow the Fund to carry out an important signalling function; a government which received approval for its standstill would suffer relatively little damage to its reputation, while the possibility that the Fund would not approve would discourage governments from utilizing the option strategically. Naturally, the IMF should limit its *ex-ante* advice to the debtor government and share its opinion with the markets only *ex post* so as to avoid inciting a panic. A definitive reinterpretation of Article VIII(2)(b) would support the IMF in this role even if it did not have legal effect in national courts. Explicit recognition by the Paris Club of an endorsed standstill would be highly desirable, if only to enhance its (informal) validity and effectiveness.

The coverage of a standstill would have to be determined case by case. It would depend on judgments about the causes of the crisis (the nature of the shock), the structure of markets, and the effects of a standstill for service of some classes of debts on the markets for others (including the interbank market) and the foreign exchange market. If the 'rush for the exits' appears likely to be a generalized stampede, then a comprehensive stay – with temporary exchange controls – may be necessary.

Strengthened IMF conditionality would reduce the likelihood that financial problems would recur. Indeed, any new money injected in conjunction with the debt restructuring, and even Fund sanction for a country's unilateral standstill, would be predicated on the government's first agreeing to fulfil stringent IMF conditions. That knowledge *ex ante* would work to minimize the likelihood of such difficulties arising in the first place. Frequent monitoring by the IMF of economic conditions in debtor countries and timely dissemination of information by the Fund would strengthen market discipline.[31]

Increased IMF resources would allow the Fund, where appropriate, to inject new money on a scale applicable to today's increasingly liquid international markets. IMF resources do not come out of thin air, of course. The question of whether such resources should be made available through an increase in IMF quotas, a new issue of SDRs, or an expansion of the resources available to the Fund through the General Arrangements to Borrow is beyond the scope of our present discussion. The point is simply that for IMF lending to have its desired stabilizing effect, loans may have to be quite significant in size, which may requiring augmenting the resources available to the Fund.

Under what conditions should the Fund supplement the workings of our proposed restructuring procedure with an injection of liquidity? The answer, we believe, does not rest on the problematic illiquidity/insolvency distinction discussed in section 2.3 above. As the Brady Plan recognized, a country with no prospect of repaying its debts fully must have its obligations written down through negotiation with the creditors. A country experiencing a temporary liquidity crisis should be able to meet it simply by stretching out the maturity structure of its debts; negotiations between the creditors and the government could back-load the payment to a time when the temporary shock producing the liquidity squeeze has disappeared. An injection of liquidity by the IMF should be provided only if one of three conditions is met:

- *The stability of the banking system is threatened.* A debt writedown or stretchout which reduces the short-run return on government obligations or leads to a rise in interest rates which aggravates the problem of non-performing loans can destabilize the debtor's banking system, creating powerful negative externalities. An injection of IMF resources may be justified to prevent the collapse of the banking system.

- *Contagion is a danger.* One rationale for the US-IMF package for Mexico was the danger that instability would spread to other developing countries and emerging markets. This is not the place to assess the evidence on contagion.[32] But neither the Bondholders Councils' nor governments in difficulty will have reason to internalize the consequences of their decisions for other investors or other countries. The IMF does have reason to be concerned about the repercussions on third parties, and it may therefore be prepared to assist; in that sense, its resources can offset this bias.[33]

- *The run is self-fulfilling.* If the Fund concludes that there is no underlying policy imbalance and the country is being subjected to a purely self-fulfilling debt run, it can either accede to the suspension of debt service and the imposition of exchange controls, or it can inject sufficient liquidity to reassure investors. Since default has costs, it may be preferable to inject liquidity. But given the difficulty of distinguishing fundamentals-based and self-fulfilling crises and of being sure that the Fund can commit in a time-consistent way to providing assistance only in response to the latter, the danger of moral hazard is great. Clearly, this is the most problematic of our three preconditions.

5.2   Alternatives and evaluation

In principle, some of these proposals could be adopted without implementing the entire package. But there are complementarities between the elements of our agenda that argue for implementing them simultaneously. For example, the recommendation that governments encourage future bond covenants to be written so that they include provisions permitting a specified majority of creditors to restructure the debt is complemented by our recommendation to establish an arbitral tribunal to which dissident creditors might appeal. The first innovation might discourage potential investors from lending if not accompanied by the second. The recommendation to strengthen IMF conditionality might not have teeth if not accompanied by an increase in Fund resources.

A less ambitious approach would limit itself to institutional innovations designed to assist the bondholders to reach agreement among themselves and with the debtor. Governments could encourage the establishment of representative committees, which would negotiate the restructuring of bonded debts in parallel with the London Club's negotiations over bank loans and the Paris Club's negotiations over official credits. They could establish an agency to provide non-binding mediation and conciliation services to facilitate agreement between the bondholders and the government. Otherwise matters would continue to proceed as at present.

This more modest approach leaves important problems unsolved. Without the creation of an agency empowered to provide binding arbitration of claims by dissident creditors, investors might be reluctant to subscribe to bond issues that made provision for a specified majority of creditors to restructure the terms of payment. Without a more active signalling role for the IMF, countries might hesitate to impose unilateral stays and would suffer severe consequences from the creditors' rush for the exits. Unless additional resources are made available to the Fund, there might be no way to inject adequate resources to prevent the collapse of the banking system with contagion to other countries. The IMF would have to be able to offer the carrot of larger loans in order effectively to wield the stick of stricter conditionality.

One way to assess the adequacy of the measures we propose is in terms of the speed with which they operate relative to the alternatives. The approach we recommend would provide a quicker resolution than the one in which third parties keep hands off, no provision is made *ex ante* for *ex-post* renegotiation and the restructuring process has to be organized from scratch. In contrast, it would work more slowly than an immediate, massive bailout from public funds.

Further bailouts along Mexican lines, however, are unlikely to be feasible because the United States will be less interested in the plight of countries further from its borders and because Congress will resist similar recourse to the Exchange Stabilization Fund. Getting the governments of the G–7 countries or the Executive Directors of the IMF to agree to finance a bailout, without other reforms, will be highly problematic. This is to compare our approach with an implausible, hypothetical alternative.

In addition, different aspects of the approach we recommend would operate at different speeds. The unilateral stay could be imposed almost instantaneously, for example. If it were necessary to inject a limited quantity of funds to prevent the banking system from collapsing, this could be done quickly by the IMF.

The idea that the Executive Board should authorize IMF officials to inject funds with the speed necessary to stabilize a country's banking system implies disbursal of at least some Fund resources without the negotiation of detailed policy conditionality. The ultimate goal of IMF lending, of course, should be to encourage policy reform. IMF loans provide governments with the breathing space they need to make the macroeconomic and regulatory adjustments required for the restoration of internal and external balance. Attaching conditionality to loans provides a financial incentive for governments to get their houses in order. It may not always be possible, however, to agree on detailed conditionality in the short period of time that modern markets permit. There may a case for limited IMF lending on the basis of relatively crude and general conditions to prevent a country's banking system from collapsing and the crisis from spreading contagiously to other countries. Only then will it be possible to hammer out the more sophisticated terms on which subsequent loans should be based. To make detailed conditionality a prerequisite for any disbursal of IMF funds is a prescription for no disbursal in response to the outbreak of crisis, which could only leave the Fund with a larger mess on its hands later.

It is worth asking how the Mexican crisis would have been handled had the mechanism we envisage been in place. To whatever degree the crisis in Mexico reflected the effects of unsustainable macroeconomic policies, we believe it was aggravated by an investor panic with self-fulfilling characteristics. The government, for which the problem was not obtaining new money but rather halting the investors' rush for the exits, would have been more inclined to suspend service on its tesobonos and cetes unilaterally had it received the assurance of the IMF that the Fund was prepared to defend that action.[34] This would have rendered it unnecessary to inject $50 billion to maintain service on those obligations. There would have been no bailout of private investors by public funds, in other words, reducing the danger of moral hazard. Of course, suspension of service on tesobonos and cetes would have had negative effects on the Mexican stock market and would still have driven up interest rates, aggravating problems of non-performing loans with damaging fallout for the country's banks. There still would have been a case for funds from the IMF to stabilize the banking system (as in Argentina in early 1995).

With a Bondholders Council and a conciliation and mediation service in place, negotiations between the creditors and the Mexican government could have commenced quickly. There is no guarantee that a mutually acceptable solution would have been reached immediately. But the provision of information about the state and future prospects of the Mexican economy by the mediation service affiliated with the Fund would have minimized disputes over the facts, while conciliation and arbitration services would have accelerated the process of reaching a settlement. It would only have been necessary to obtain approval of that settlement from a majority of the relevant class of creditors, without depriving dissident investors of the option of appealing to the arbitral tribunal. A negotiated settlement between the Bondholders Council and the Mexican government could thus have been reached which minimized damage to Mexico's international creditworthiness. Close monitoring of conditions would then have minimized the likelihood of similar difficulties arising again.

Would the crisis have been more or less likely to spill over to other emerging markets than actually was the case in early 1995? A unilateral stay on tesobonos, even if the policy had been endorsed by the IMF and led to the quick initiation of restructuring negotiations, would surely have had negative repercussions for investor confidence in other emerging markets. There would have been a need for the IMF to provide financial assistance to other countries, as it did for Argentina. The negative fallout elsewhere in Latin America and the need for IMF assistance might have been greater than was the case with the extension of the $50 billion loan from the United States and the IMF to Mexico. But we have suggested reasons why a more orderly procedure, known in advance, would limit contagion.

In any case, a massive bailout is not the relevant comparison. Comparable loans will not be extended in the future, both because of political resistance in the G–7 countries and because of the serious dangers of moral hazard to which they give rise for foreign investors and the governments concerned. The relevant comparison is with present institutions and no loan, or present institutions and an IMF loan on a much smaller scale. It is virtually certain that contagion would have been much more severe in such a scenario than in the presence of the institutional reforms sketched here.

6   Conclusion

Financial distress normally results from a real shock or bad policies, both of which have real costs. The desirable distribution of that burden between debtor and creditors and among different classes of the latter involves political considerations that are beyond the scope of this report. Nevertheless, we should note that circumstances have changed significantly since the early period of the 1980s debt crisis, when it could be argued that there was a significant systemic risk associated with the exposure of major banks, which could therefore not be permitted to 'take the hit'.

The development of emerging markets in the bonds and equities of developing countries is a mixed blessing. The fact that debt is widely held by mutual funds, pension funds and individuals means that losses can be absorbed and unserviceable debts can be and are written down without jeopardizing the stability of creditor-country financial institutions. It means that good news can have powerful effects: new investors in search of yield may be prepared to jump quickly into emerging markets when credible policy reforms are put in place, notwithstanding a history of debt servicing difficulties. The innovations we propose are perhaps more appropriate and more feasible in such an environment.

At the same time, the speed with which markets move and the large number of investors mean that bad news, or even the possibility of bad news, creates problems of collective action even more serious than those of the 1980s. Bad news can provoke a powerful rush for the exits, with devastating effects on the debtor in the short run and potentially adverse consequences for other developing-country debtors.

The best way to deal with bad news is to prevent it. The best way of managing financial crises in highly indebted countries is to prevent them from happening in the first place. More comprehensive and timely IMF surveillance can send unambiguous early-warning signals of impending difficulties. Linking the availability of IMF support to the regular release of information can strengthen market discipline.

Even under these circumstances, however, it is still possible for unanticipated contingencies to intervene and financial difficulties to arise. The Mexican crisis, one of the first full-blown crises in the new era of bond and equity finance, has exposed the inadequacies of current procedures for dealing with them. This realization has prompted a variety of proposals for institutional reform.

Our analysis points to significant problems with each of the popular reform proposals. Each of these schemes, however, has desirable features, and current procedures have decided limitations. This leads us to recommend modest but potentially important reform in a number of directions. The IMF should more actively transmit signals about the advisability of unilateral suspensions. One or more bondholders' committees should be formed, and their authority should be recognized by creditor-country governments. A mediation and conciliation service should be established to provide information to all parties and to speed negotiations between private creditors and the debtor. Loan contracts and bond covenants should specify that a majority of creditors be entitled to alter the terms of the debt agreement and that objections would be referred to a dedicated tribunal to prevent the tribunal's findings from being disputed in court. The resources of the IMF should be increased to allow the Fund, where appropriate, to inject new money on the requisite scale. IMF conditionality should be strengthened in order to reduce the likelihood that financial problems will recur.

This is not an ideal solution. As Calvo and Goldstein (1995) conclude, there is no magic bullet for solving the problems raised by sovereign debt. But there is much to be done. Our proposals, if adopted, would represent a significant advance over the *status quo*.

As the experience of economies in transition has reminded us, markets are *social institutions*: they function properly only within a well-defined legal and institutional framework. Some of these institutions can develop spontaneously, in a decentralized fashion; others must be created by concerted action. Thus helping to construct the framework is not inappropriate official intervention in the market place, but rather helping the market to work (what in post-war German economic policy analysis is called *Ordnungspolitik*). We hope that the proposals here may contribute to that effort.

Notes

For comments on earlier drafts, the authors are grateful to Raquel Fernandez, Zanny Minton-Beddoes, Dani Rodrik, David Vines and Charles Wyplosz, as well as numerous helpful officials who were vigorous and constructive critics. We are indebted also to Giovanni Vitale for excellent research assistance and to Eleanor Burke and Anitra Hume-Wright for their help and support in producing the manuscript under severe time pressure.

1. This interpretation of the market's reaction is not uncontroversial. Below we analyse the conditions under which this kind of market failure – known as the creditors' 'rush for the exits' – can arise. This problem of over-reaction by creditors in response to disturbances is related to the possibility of over-lending during the preceding period owing to, *inter alia*, principal-agent problems between underwriting banks and their clients (Darity and Horn, 1988), implicit default-risk guarantees offered by the authorities (McKinnon and Pill, 1995), and excessive enthusiasm on the part of the lenders (Krugman, 1995). It is not the purpose of this report to analyse the validity of these arguments. Our point is only to note that the identification of some market failure is necessary to justify the call for institutional reform.

2. Instead, the US government and the IMF provided a large loan to finance the maintenance of debt service. Significant portions were used to retire maturing debt ('to bail out the creditors', in the words of some critics).

3. Some commentators prefer to invoke Chapter 9, which allows an insolvent municipal government to petition for reorganization in bankruptcy.

4. Obviously, there are practical problems of determining which countries should be subject to these provisions, such as whether the high-income industrial nations as well as developing countries should submit to the authority of any new international entity, and whether these procedures would extend to countries whose debts were largely denominated in domestic currency or held by domestic residents. We consider these issues below.

5. French bankruptcy law similarly permits the court to impose a reorganization plan without the approval of creditors (Mitchell, 1990).

6. The receiver can, however, usually obtain an indemnity from the creditors.

7. Cohen (1985) argues that solvency for a country is a function of the same basic parameters as for a firm, notably forecasts of the rate of growth of revenues (GDP, exports, or public sector receipts) and of the interest rate.

8. See our discussion of Paris and London Club procedures below.

9. The Maxwell case, where the firm had significant assets in both the United States and the United Kingdom, appears to raise the question of competing jurisdictions. The UK administrator sought control of the Chapter 11 reorganization of the US subsidiary. The outcome clarified the point that the assets are subject to the jurisdiction of the host country, but the management of those assets (the debtor in possession) was under the ownership and hence the control of a UK company, so the UK administrator did have control. Our point is not significantly weakened.

10. The Roosevelt Administration attached priority to the reconstruction of international trade and refused to use sanctions as leverage on behalf of private investors.

11. This is despite the shift of bargaining power somewhat towards the creditors since the inter-war period. In earlier periods it was common for a sovereign borrower to insist that its own law should be the 'proper law' of the debt contract (as recognized by the Permanent Court of International Justice in the 1927 Case Concerning Certain Serbian and Brazilian Loans). Foreign investors in Latin America were normally required to accept a 'Calvo clause', which specified that the proper law was the local law and waived recourse to diplomatic protection. Individual investors wishing to go into sovereign countries had little leverage. Now large banks and mutual funds have greater weight in the international capital markets, and such intermediaries can and do insist that the proper law should be that of the creditor's state or a third 'forum' state (usually a major financial centre) and that the courts of that country should have jurisdiction in any dispute.

12. Whether this protracted interruption is properly attributable to the shortcomings of the renegotiation process is an open question. One interpretation is that a speedier, more successful conclusion to negotiations would have allowed the resumption of international lending in the 1930s and encouraged the establishment of an international financial environment free of capital controls after the second world war. An alternative view is that governments had moved so far in a dirigiste direction owing to the experience of the Great Depression that they would have suppressed transactions on capital account in any case following the second world war.

13. Except in so far as there is reason to worry about the reputational repercussions of unilateral suspension (a point to which we return below) and the short-run effects on financing trade.

14. The potential role of bondholders' committees is reinforced, however, by experience in the restructurings of bonded debt triggered by repayment difficulties in the 1980s. Panama and Nigeria both defaulted on bonded debt in this period. In neither case did restructurings involve negotiations with official bondholders' committees, although settlement offers were made only after informal contacts with substantial bondholders (Fernandez-Ansola and Laursen, 1995). Debtor countries' unilateral offers were final, and bondholders signalled their approval by exchanging old instruments for new ones. Significantly, in both of these cases the offer was made only after an extended period of default, and the exchange of old instruments for new ones took six to twelve months to complete. There is evidence, therefore, that the process suffered from the absence of formal representation. The cases of Costa Rica and Guatemala, which restructured their bonds as they matured, are rather similar.

15. The first meeting of the London Club was held to reschedule Zaire's debt in 1976.

16. When exceptions were made, as with Peru in 1976, they ultimately served to ensure that almost all subsequent bank negotiations were contingent on IMF agreements. In Brazil's Brady Plan settlement, the banks did proceed without an IMF programme in place (though the Fund did not object).

17. See the discussion below of the Allied Bank case.

18. In the case of Russia, the government contacted foreign trade officials of each creditor country, who appointed a bank to represent the interests of all creditors in that country. Then the ten largest creditors formed a 'Forum of Trade Credit Groups' which negotiates with the Russian authorities. Procedures are similar to the London Club, and restructuring follows Paris Club terms ('comparable treatment'). The Forum cannot commit any creditor, and creditors have a simple 'take it or leave it' option – which they normally accept, because there is a 'no better terms' clause. This approach works far from perfectly, however; in the case of Russia, the defaults that occurred are still outstanding three years later.

19. Recall that one of the conditions identified by Krugman and Taylor (1978) for a contractionary or destabilizing devaluation was significant quantities of foreign-currency-denominated debt.

20. This is one advantage of UK law, which allows creditors a lien on local government revenue (in contrast to Chapter 9 in the United States).

21. We address the problem of effective collateralization below.

22. Orange County hoped for some time that the State of California would eventually bail it out. A different kind of interplay between central governments and public entities proved disastrous in the CFA countries of West Africa, where state-owned enterprises (SOEs) borrowed abroad, then the governments borrowed from the SOEs; when the governments could not meet their obligations, the SOEs could not repay the banks, and banking systems collapsed.

23. The same argument is made, *a fortiori*, in respect of 'imposed' measures: closing the courts to 'rogue' creditors and some kind of 'international bankruptcy court'.

24. An example is the Allied Bank litigation in the United States, in which the Appeals Court ultimately vacated its initial decision that relied on the act of state doctrine to block the claim of a creditor dissenting against the Costa Rica resettlement package (Greenwood and Mercer, 1995, and Hurlock, 1995). The reversal followed an *amicus curiae* brief from the Department of Justice arguing that New York would suffer as a financial centre (and thus the United States as a 'forum state') if lenders could not enforce contracts. This illustrates a very important point regarding the incentives and domestic pressures facing creditor governments – and a major qualification to the bankruptcy analogy – namely, that a change in national bankruptcy law is unlikely to attract or repel international business, whereas a change in sovereign immunity rules is likely to lead to immediate migration of business away from financial centres with an unattractively broad view of sovereign immunity. Transactors would simply choose another 'proper law' for contracts. Lenders and lawyers compete for business – a UK bank will prefer UK law as the proper law of a loan contract, and clearly UK legal firms will as well. So they would oppose any move of this kind by the United Kingdom, and such opposition would appear in other countries too.

25. It should be noted that in most national codes, that role is limited; the court provides a framework for negotiations, and the judge keeps them within the provisions of the code. That does not go at all as far as proposing a settlement, the terms of a writedown, etc. – that is for direct negotiations between debtor and creditor, with the judge possibly empowered to require dissident creditors to accept it (or worse).

26. To prevent dissident creditors from racing to court, this might require sanction by the IMF for the imposition of exchange controls, which would have to be supported by a broad interpretation of Article VIII(2)(b).

27. Indeed, tesobonos are currently not counted as external debt according to conventional measures.

28. One solution to this problem is to establish the facility through an amendment to the IMF Articles, which would override the efforts of governments to exempt their debts from its authority. But such an amendment would still have to be implemented through changes in national law. In addition, as mentioned above, amending the Articles of Agreement is difficult in practice. It also seems unlikely that the governments of the leading creditor countries would readily agree to such an amendment.

29. While coordination between the Paris and London Clubs has been extensive, it has been less than perfect, as in the case of Poland, Liberia, Togo, Costa Rica and the Dominican Republic (1978–85), where it was difficult to reach 'comparable treatment'. In the case of Zaire (1976–9), the official creditors had to threaten the suspension of their rescheduling in order to get the banks to negotiate. There is a danger of exacerbating problems of coordination through the creation of a new entity.

30. While new debts would be automatically referred to the tribunal for arbitration, pre-existing debts might not (since there would be no provision in the bond covenant for arbitration), implying that this innovation would have to be phased in over time.

31. Rodrik (1995b) asks why multilateral institutions like the IMF should have a comparative advantage relative to the markets in monitoring economic conditions in borrowing countries. His answer rests on the public-good character of information: that each potential lender has an incentive to gather additional information only to the point where the benefits to that lender match the costs, but this information could be passed on to other potential lenders at zero incremental cost. Hence there is a need for a multilateral institution operating in the public interest to internalize this externality.

32. A review of some evidence is in Calvo and Reinhart (1995). We have a few words to say on this question in the concluding section.

33. It can be argued that creating a procedure for orderly workouts through the adoption of the other elements of our proposal could itself reduce the danger of contagion, which would then reduce the need for active use of the IMF facility.

34. A frequent objection to this possibility is that a suspension of debt service by Mexico would have induced other developing countries to emulate its example, returning to the 'statist, inward-looking policies' of earlier years (Calvo and Goldstein, 1995). We follow these authors in concluding that this scenario is implausible.

References

Aghion, P., Hart O. and Moore, J. (1992), 'The Economics of Bankruptcy Reform', *Journal of Law, Economics and Organization* 8, pp. 523–46.

Bordo, M. and Eichengreen, B. (1993), *A Retrospective on the Bretton Woods System*, Chicago, University of Chicago Press.

Calvo, G. (1988), 'Servicing the Public Debt: The Role of Expectations', *American Economic Review* 78, pp. 647–61.

Calvo, G. and Goldstein, M. (1995), 'Crisis Prevention and Crisis Management After Mexico: What Role for the Official Sector?', unpublished manuscript, University of Maryland and Institute for International Economics.

Calvo, S. and Reinhart, C.M. (1995), 'Capital Inflows to Latin America: Is There Evidence of Contagion Effects?', unpublished manuscript, The World Bank and International Monetary Fund.

Cline, W.R. (1989), 'The Baker Plan and Brady Reformulation: An Evaluation', in I. Husain and I. Diwan (eds.), *Dealing with the Debt Crisis*, Washington D.C., The World Bank, pp. 176–93.

Cohen, D. (1985), 'How to Evaluate the Solvency of an Indebted Nation', *Economic Policy* 1, pp. 139–67.

Cornelli, F. and Felli, L. (1995), 'Bankruptcy Theory and Mechanism Design', this volume.

Darity, W.M. Jr. and Horn, B.L. (1988), *The Loan Pushers: The Role of Commercial Banks in the International Debt Crisis*, Cambridge, Mass., Ballinger Publishing.

Diamond, D. and Dybvig, P. (1983), 'Bank Runs, Deposit Insurance and Liquidity', *Journal of Political Economy* 91, pp. 401–19.

Eichengreen, B. and Portes, R. (1987), 'The Anatomy of Financial Crises', in R. Portes and A. Swoboda (eds.), *Threats to International Financial Stability*, Cambridge, Cambridge University Press, pp. 10–57.

Eichengreen, B. and Portes, R. (1989a), 'Dealing with Debt: The 1930s and the 1980s', in I. Husain and I. Diwan (eds), *Dealing with the Debt Crisis*, Washington D.C., The World Bank, pp. 69–88.

Eichengreen, B. and Portes, R. (1989b), 'After the Deluge: Default, Negotiation and Readjustment during the Interwar Years', in B. Eichengreen and P. Lindert (eds), *The International Debt Crisis in Historical Perspective*, Cambridge, Mass., MIT Press, pp. 12–47.

Eichengreen, B., Rose, A. and Wyplosz, C. (1994), 'Is There a Safe Passage to EMU?', CEPR Discussion Paper No. 1061.

Favero, C., Giavazzi, F., and Spaventa, L. (1995), 'Spreads on Italian Bonds', paper presented to CEPR European Summer Symposium in International Macroeconomic, Perugia.

Fernandez-Ansola, J.J. and Laursen, T. (1995), 'Historical Experience with Bond Financing to Developing Countries', unpublished manuscript, International Monetary Fund.

Fishlow, A. (1989), 'Conditionality and Willingness to Pay: Evidence from the 1890s', in B. Eichengreen and P. Lindert (eds), *The International Debt Crisis in Historical Perspective*, Cambridge, Mass., MIT Press, pp. 86–105.

Franks, J. (1995), 'Some Issues in Sovereign Debt and Distressed Reorganizations', this volume.

Franks, J. and Nyborg, K. (1994), 'Control Rights and the Loss of Private Benefits: The Case of the UK Insolvency Code', CEPR/ESF Working Paper No. 47.

Franks, J., Nyborg, K. and Torous, W. (1995), 'A Comparison of US, UK and German Insolvency Codes', unpublished manuscript, London Business School and UCLA.

Franks, J. and Torous, W. (1989), 'An Empirical Investigation of US Firms in Reorganization', *Journal of Finance* 44, pp. 747–69.

Franks, J. and Torous, W. (1994), 'How Shareholders and Creditors Fare in Workouts and Chapter 11 Reorganizations', *Journal of Financial Economics* 35, pp. 349–70.

Giavazzi, F. and Pagano, M. (1990), 'Confidence Crises and Public Debt Management', in R. Dornbusch and M. Draghi (eds), *Public Debt Management: Theory and History*, Cambridge, Cambridge University Press, pp. 125–43.

Greenwood, C. and Mercer, H. (1995), 'Considerations of International Law', this volume.

Helpman, E. (1988), 'Voluntary Debt Reduction: Incentives and Welfare', NBER Working Paper No. 2692.

Hurlock, J.B. (1995), 'Sovereign Bankruptcies: Countries Cannot Always Pay', unpublished manuscript, White & Case.

Jensen, M. (1992), 'Corporate Control and the Politics of Finance', in E. Altman (ed.), *Bankruptcy and Distressed Restructurings*, New York, Irwin, pp. 3–43.

Klingen, C. (1995), 'How Private Creditors Fared with Sovereign Lending: Evidence from the 1970–1992 Period', paper presented at CEPR Workshop Political Economy, Sovereign Debt and the IMF, Cambridge 7/8 July.

Krugman, P. (1988), 'Financing versus Forgiving a Debt Overhang: Some Analytic Notes', *Journal of Development Economics* 29, pp. 79–100.

Krugman, P. (1995), 'Dutch Tulips and Emerging Markets', *Foreign Affairs* 74, pp. 28–44.

Krugman, P. and Taylor, L. (1978), 'Contractionary Effects of Devaluations', *Journal of International Economics* 8, pp. 445–56.

Lindert, P. and Morton, P. (1990), 'How Sovereign Debt has Worked', in J.D. Sachs (ed.), *Developing Country Debt and Economic Performance* 1, Chicago and London, The University of Chicago Press, pp. 33–105.

LoPucki, L. and Whitford, W. (1992), 'Corporate Governance in the Bankruptcy Reorganization of Large, Publicly-Held Companies', unpublished manuscript, University of Wisconsin.

McKinnon, R. and Pill, H. (1995), 'Credible Liberalizations and International Capital Flows', unpublished manuscript, Stanford University.

Macmillan, R. (1995), 'New Lease of Life for Bondholder Councils', *Financial Times*, 15 August, p. 11.

Mann, F.A. (1992), *The Legal Aspect of Money: With Special Reference to Comparative Private and Public International Law*, Oxford, Oxford University Press.

Marston, R. (1993), 'Interest Differentials under Bretton Woods and the post-Bretton Woods Float', in M. Bordo and B. Eichengreen, pp. 515–46.

Mitchell, J. (1990), 'The Economics of Bankruptcy in Reforming Socialist Economies', unpublished manuscript, Cornell University.

Obstfeld, M. (1993), 'The Adjustment Mechanism', in M. Bordo and B. Eichengreen, pp. 201–68.

Rieffel, A. (1985), 'The Role of the Paris Club in Managing Debt Problems', *Princeton Essays in International Finance* 161, International Finance Division, Department of Economics, Princeton University.

Rodrik, D. (1995a), 'Getting Interventions Right: How South Korea and Taiwan Grew Rich', *Economic Policy* 20, pp. 55–97.

Rodrik, D. (1995b), 'Why is There Multilateral Lending?', CEPR Discussion Paper No. 1207.

Sachs, J.D. (1995), 'Do We Need an International Lender of Last Resort?', unpublished manuscript, Harvard University.

Sachs, J.D., Tornell, A. and Velasco, A. (1995), 'Lessons from Mexico', unpublished manuscript, Harvard University.

Schwartz, A.J. (1995), 'Comments on The Collapse of the Mexican Peso and Do We Need an International Lender of Last Resort?', unpublished manuscript, National Bureau of Economic Research.

Sessions, G.A. (1992), *Prophesying Upon the Bones: J. Reuben Clark and the Foreign Debt Crisis, 1933–39*, Urbana and Chicago, University of Illinois Press.

Shleifer, A. and Summers, L. (1988), 'Breach of Trust in Hostile Takeovers', in A. Auerbach (ed.), *Corporate Takeovers: Causes and Consequences*, Chicago, University of Chicago Press, pp. 33–56.

Sussman, O. (1994), 'Talking About Growth: The Evolution of Contractual Language', unpublished manuscript, Hebrew University.

von Hagen, J. (1991), 'A Note on the Empirical Effectiveness of Formal Fiscal Restraints', *Journal of Public Economics* 44, pp. 199–210.

Weiss, L. (1990), 'Bankruptcy Resolution: Direct Costs and Violation of Absolute Priority', *Journal of Financial Economics* 27, pp. 285–314.

Wynne, W.H. (1951), *State Insolvency and Foreign Bondholders*, New Haven, Yale University Press.

Annex 1

The theory of bankruptcy and mechanism design

Francesca Cornelli
London Business School and CEPR

Leonardo Felli
London School of Economics

1　The need for a bankruptcy procedure

The design of a bankruptcy procedure for a firm in financial distress or a country which is unable to service its foreign-currency-denominated debts is not an easy task. Such a procedure may not even be desirable. There are two main reasons for this. First, in a world in which contracting parties are fully rational and can forecast every future contingency and specify them without any significant cost in a comprehensive contract (in jargon in a world of 'complete contracts'), no purpose is served by a bankruptcy law.

Consider two individuals engaging in a business transaction. When they write the contract they can forecast all the relevant future contingencies, including all possible causes of default for either party, and specify in the credit contract what the parties should do in each contingency. For example, the two parties could write in their contract exactly the same provisions as a bankruptcy law, if they considered this to be suitable, or alternatively a debtor could write provisions in a contract with one creditor which differ from those in a contract with another creditor. In general, provided the contract is enforceable and binding, there is no need for a law that tells the parties what to do, but simply an authority (in the case of international debt, a supra-national authority) which guarantees the enforcement of their preferred contract. Given the greater flexibility of a contract with respect to a law (a contract can always be tailored more closely to the transaction at hand), the contractual solution will in general dominate the legal procedure. Hence in an international environment it would suffice to guarantee that contracts, say between a government and a foreign investor, are enforced by some international organization. No other provision will be required.

The second reason is that the *ex-post* spontaneous negotiation between the parties will lead to the efficient outcome, even if, for some unforeseen reason, the parties find themselves in a situation for which they did not make provision in the original contract. Indeed, when ownership rights on the relevant assets are clearly defined, it is not clear (at least theoretically) why the *ex-post* bargaining among the parties would not be the ideal solution to the default problem. This is certainly the case in a world in which information is perfect and individuals are perfectly rational. In such a context we know that *ex-post* bargaining is always efficient. This implies that the 'Coasian' bargaining among debtors and creditors (or in general among all parties involved) will always bring them to the Pareto frontier where it is simply a matter of distribution, and this would be the only aspect with which a bankruptcy procedure would have to deal.

Obviously the situations described above are far from being a realistic description of a creditor-debtor arrangement. It is important, however, to identify factors that alter these situations. First, forecasting all contingencies is impossible, mainly because some individuals are less informed than others. Second, writing contracts – when the transaction concerned involves big stakes, such as a country's borrowing from either private or public foreign investors – is not a simple and costless task, especially if they have to specify every possible contingency that may occur in the future. Third, there is always a considerable amount of uncertainty and asymmetry of information regarding who has claims on a particular asset.[1] Finally, because of the difficulty of processing all the information, considerable delays may occur and a lot of resources may be wasted in the effort to decide the final allocation. These problems make a bankruptcy procedure desirable. Moreover, how a bankruptcy procedure performs, hence what is the optimal bankruptcy procedure, may be measured by assessing how the procedure reduces the efficiency costs associated with such problems.

In the context of our analysis an essential question is whether some of these problems are bigger in the case of a country borrowing, for example, from foreign private investors than in the corporate case. Indeed, in an international context the asymmetric information problems seem even worse. It is certainly harder for the creditors to access certified and monitored sources of information concerning the financial health of the investments undertaken by the borrowing country. It may be difficult to assess the political strength of the government or the priority in the government agenda of foreign debt service, especially when weighed against the ruling party's priority of, say, maximizing the probability of re-election. In other words the international framework seems to us to be an environment in which the inefficiencies created by transaction and information costs are magnified.

An additional reason for questioning the viability of a bankruptcy provision – even in the very limited sense of this term when contracts are complete – is whether there are any tools to enforce an international procedure. More specifically, a bankruptcy procedure in corporate law is mainly concerned with the problem of allocating among the creditors the assets of the firm in financial distress. The question then is what are the 'assets' in an international framework? Is there anything that can play the role of assets, or more generally is there any mechanism that would require the parties to the international transaction to comply, at least partially, with the original debt contract? Note that a bankruptcy procedure in corporate law makes no provision in the clearly unusual event of a firm with no assets whatsoever. No bankruptcy problems arise in this case.

In the case of a sovereign debt default, however, it is highly likely that we will end up in a situation where there are no assets to seize. We address this issue in the following manner. First, we assume that there is no collateral (no asset to seize) and we ask whether a reputation argument can make the commitment to submit to a binding arbitration procedure time-consistent. Second, we ask whether it is possible to identify and set a collateral that can be seized in an international debt situation. Finally, using the framework constructed we propose some of the desirable features of an optimal bankruptcy procedure in the context of sovereign debt.

Before proceeding, however, we have to identify the basic tension between *ex-ante* and *ex-post* efficiency which determines the optimal choice of collateral.[2] This is equivalent to identifying the desirable goals of a bankruptcy procedure. The most relevant goals are represented by *ex-ante* efficiency considerations. In other words, a bankruptcy procedure should provide the proper incentives to both the creditors and the manager of the debt (the government, in this case) even before default occurs. When examining a bankruptcy procedure in the corporate law context, another order of efficiency consideration is represented by *ex-post* efficiency considerations associated with identifying best possible uses and allocations of the assets in place at the moment of the default. These *ex-post* efficiency considerations take a different form in the context of a government borrowing from foreign investors. We start with these latter efficiency considerations and identify the features they suggest for an 'optimal' bankruptcy procedure. We then proceed to analyse the features suggested by the *ex-ante* efficiency considerations.

2 Bankruptcy without collateral

We will consider first what happens in the absence of any 'asset' in a sovereign debt situation. If the transaction is repeated in the future and the debtor needs to borrow from the same source, the creditor will have a tool to enforce at least the partial payment of the past debts: the threat not to lend additional funds. This problem is analysed in the literature on sovereign debt (see Eaton and Fernandez, 1994, for a survey of this literature). A similar threat could be successful even if the debtor country does not plan to borrow from the same source in the future, if the information concerning previous defaults is available to new creditors. This could be the main role of a bankruptcy procedure when no 'assets' or any form of collateral are available: to facilitate that a sovereign country establish a reputation for servicing debt and to provide widespread information concerning countries that impair their reputation by defaulting on existing debt contracts. The problem of enforcement and deterrence involves not only the deterrence to default, but also the incentive to behave according to the previously agreed rules in case the default has taken place. We will return to this issue when we discuss the role of renegotiation in bankruptcy.

It is worth asking whether some of the problems highlighted by the literature on corporate bankruptcy are associated with the existence of collateral, in which case the problem might disappear when no collateral is available. Consider, for example, the often mentioned drawback that some bankruptcy procedures (such as receivership in the United Kingdom) induce 'excessive liquidation'. Does this problem disappear when no collateral exists? We do not think so. The absence of collateral does not imply that there is no danger of excessive liquidation. Imagine that the borrowing that created the debt has been used to finance a project which is now only partially completed. At this stage the project is worth very little, let us assume for simplicity it is worth zero, but if more money is invested it will be worth a positive amount. The debtor, however, is in a liquidity crisis, and needs more financing; at the same time it is now clear that the creditors will never be able to recover their entire initial investment. For the creditors as a whole it would be best to refinance the project so that they will get back at least part of their initial investment (in addition to their added capital). But if the creditors do not feel sufficiently protected by the bankruptcy law they may decide not to refinance. An example in the corporate world is the case of Canary Wharf in London. Although it was clear that the creditors would never have got back all their initial investment, they nonetheless decided to add more money, bring the project to completion and sell the properties. In absence of a bankruptcy law that allowed them to take control of the remaining part of the process, however, they might have decided otherwise.

In this context excessive liquidation may occur because a project is not refinanced, and is therefore liquidated, even if it was optimal to keep it going. The absence of collateral is thus not enough to avoid excessive liquidation, which may arise from the creditor's failure to raise additional funds for the project. Various situations may arise depending on the value of the assets. It is important to identify in each case which types of assets are involved. For example, international debt very often involves the financing of large projects which may have no particular value unless they are completed. In general, the growth of an entire country may be slowed down if it is cut out of the international capital markets as a consequence of its default. Because of the nature of the assets usually financed by this type of lending, the problem of 'excessive liquidation' and economically inefficient decisions undertaken because of the default is particularly disruptive.

3   The optimal design of a bankruptcy

Assume now that a collateral exists. In the absence of complete contracts it is useful to ask what features characterize an 'optimal' bankruptcy procedure in the context of a country borrowing from foreign investors.

3.1   *Ex-post* efficiency

In the corporate context, *ex-post* efficiency implies that an activity (a set of investments) should be continued if its continuation value is higher than its liquidation value. Furthermore, the project should be placed in the hands of those who value it most. The first criterion applies also in the international context, but it is not clear whether the second applies when sovereignty problems are considered. Even if an investment has a higher value in the hands of foreign owners, it is not necessarily desirable to let them take it over, at least from the point of view of the government of the debtor country. Of course in a world with perfect information and perfectly competitive markets the foreign buyers would be willing to pay enough to compensate for any sovereignty loss. But if information is imperfect and parties derive private benefits from control, the markets might not generate the necessary compensations to the sovereign country (see Cornelli and Li, 1994, for an example).

Finally, in the corporate context *ex-post* considerations are mainly concerned with how to restructure the credits. These considerations involve the decision whether or not to liquidate the company and, if it is continued, how to restructure it. This last point concerns the choice of a new ownership structure as well as a redefinition of the operations of the company. Here a bankruptcy procedure in the case of sovereign debtors has much less scope. First, liquidation is not a choice; and second, the possibilities for restructuring are much more limited. It is true that a country may be required to discuss its economic plans before the crisis is solved – and that could be analogous to restructuring the activity of a firm – but the choice of a new ownership structure is definitely more limited. Creditors may come to possess some of the country's assets but not much more than that. This is quite different from corporate bankruptcy law, where general creditors are seen as the firm's residual owners (see Baird and Picker, 1991). We will return to this point when discussing how a bankruptcy procedure may provide a debtor with the necessary *ex-ante* incentives.

In the context of sovereign debt a reinterpretation of the *ex-post* efficiency criterion becomes relevant. In fact, one of the main roles of a collateral in a bankruptcy procedure is to provide the creditors with a threat that keeps in line the incentives of the debtor (*ex-ante* efficiency considerations). When choosing the appropriate collateral, however, *ex-post* or allocative efficiency considerations play a role. Some forms of seizure of assets are worse than others in terms of economic efficiency. We must remember that the creditor is trying to seize assets from a country which is not necessarily in its best possible state (since it has just defaulted). What might be right as a punishment could be very costly from other points of view. For example, it might entail stripping down and stopping other projects that are important for the development of the country. Even if the *ex-ante* considerations are important, we must be careful not to impose a mechanism that is too costly in terms of *ex-post* efficiency. The right balance between these two objectives should provide the optimal bankruptcy procedure. Therefore *ex-post* efficiency considerations, redefined as we propose, are no less important in a sovereign debt environment than in a corporate environment.

Also relevant to *ex-post* efficiency is the question of whether the problem at the root of the default is permanent or temporary. This aspect is central to the issue discussed below: whether renegotiation should be discouraged. In this respect, the distinction between financial distress and insolvency is important. We define financial distress as a situation where cash flows are insufficient to cover current obligations. Insolvency could refer either to stock value (that is to cases in which the present value of the firm's cash flows is less than its total obligations) or to flows (that is to cases which coincide with financial distress or illiquidity). Note that a firm could be insolvent on a stock basis but not on a flow basis, in which case creditors would have little power. Then a bankruptcy procedure would give the debtor the incentive to begin restructuring even before it is obliged to do so by its creditors. This distinction is important because many of the delays and difficulties in a bankruptcy procedure are due to the information problems associated with determining whether a firm is insolvent or only illiquid.

Such problems are exacerbated when considering a sovereign debt situation. In principle, it is not even clear what we mean by insolvency in this context. If it is difficult to establish the net worth of a firm, it is almost impossible to do it for a country. In fact, it is always possible to find a rate of growth high enough for the country to become solvent at a certain point. The question should therefore be whether the country will become solvent in a reasonable amount of time and with a satisfactory interval of confidence, in order to avoid unrealistically optimistic forecasts and too long delays. This is extremely difficult to forecast. An easier and more accessible forecast would require a solvency assessment not on the entire country, but rather on some specific project which is more closely connected to the debt.[3] This alternative approach would be useful since in other cases the distinction between illiquidity and insolvency would become untenable. The distinction is crucial when deciding, for example, whether to discontinue or refinance some activities or simply to delay the repayment, or to make the creditors the new owners. The latter choice is never an issue in an international context, while the former is important only if we consider specific projects and not an entire country.

In view of the above, a collateral should be chosen that makes the punishment harsh enough to have a deterrent effect on the debtor, but that is not very distortionary so as to preserve allocative efficiency. This could take the form of a deposit with the IMF. This type of collateral has a strong punishment component and at the same time does not require the destruction of productive assets. The problem would be whether it is realistic for a country that relies heavily on capital imports from abroad to post such a bond, since it would mean freezing funds that could be used for productive purposes.

If providing the capital is difficult there could be other alternatives. One possibility is to ask the country in question to put up as a collateral bonds issued by its own private firms. As long as the country is not defaulting, the interest payments would keep accruing to the government; but if the country defaults, the creditors could seize the bonds, and the foreign investors would become creditors of the private firms. The original credit contract would therefore become a standard credit contract between two private firms in two different countries. In this case the foreign creditors' claim will be guaranteed by the internal corporate bankruptcy procedure of the debtor country, hence the efficiency properties of the procedure will be relevant as well. In other words, if this type of collateral is chosen, an efficient internal bankruptcy procedure in the debtor country will be critical for the country's ability to raise foreign funds. No regulation would be necessary to achieve this goal, since all the incentives are in place for the debtor country to improve the efficiency of its internal bankruptcy procedure.

Alternatively, a country could use as collateral shares of domestic firms it owns (provided that such firms are in good health). Of course in the case of default there is always the possibility that a country might refuse to honour such shares and bonds, but this would raise the stakes of the default decision since it would create problems for the domestic firms. Moreover, if the debtor country also manages to default on the private bonds used as collateral it would be possible to envisage stronger punishments (this time more distortionary in terms of allocative efficiency). In this way the first role of the collateral (compensating the creditors at least partially) would be detached from the second role (deterrence) which could be accomplished by 'out of path' punishments.

3.2   *Ex-ante* incentives for creditors

We turn now to *ex-ante* efficiency considerations. One of the objectives of a bankruptcy procedure is to avoid letting creditors enter into a grab race. If creditors are allowed to seize assets before an agreement has been reached, the free-rider problem means they will end up damaging themselves as a group. Bankruptcy imposes an automatic stay on creditors. Then it may be understood as a forum in which parties negotiate with each other. A bankruptcy procedure, therefore, could be interpreted as a multilateral bargaining procedure among all the parties involved. Such bargaining may lead to the replacement of the management and the reorganization of the existing resources if this is in the interests of the parties. The final allocation will depend on the relative bargaining power of the various parties. This depends on both the outside options of each party (a creditor can at any time threaten to leave with something it is entitled to) and the structure of the negotiation (who has the right to make offers, who is entitled to respond, in which order, and so on). It can be said that a bankruptcy procedure is imposing an extensive form on the bargaining process and is specifying the outside options of the parties involved. Both the extensive form and the outside options are fundamental in determining what each party will receive in the end and therefore will affect *ex-ante* the incentives of the various parties.

For example, a bankruptcy procedure should provide the debtor with the incentive to maximize the profits of the project financed, but it should also provide creditors with the incentive to lend their funds at a reasonable rate. Creditors will lend on better conditions if they feel they will be adequately protected in the case of default, and in general capital markets work better. Explicit *ex-ante* recognition that countries might not repay 100% of their debt may, in principle, worsen market terms by revealing to investors an additional source of risk. The possibility of default is already implicitly taken into account, however, when an interest rate higher than the risk-free rate is applied. Lenders evaluate the country risk and the possibility of default and raise the interest rate accordingly. Hence the availability of a workout procedure may not reveal any more information than that already priced by the market in the higher interest rate.

The fact that some internationally recognized workout procedure has been adopted should help reduce the uncertainty and problems that arise in the case of default. Lenders will know how situations of default will evolve, how they will be protected and what they will ultimately be able to obtain. Facing less uncertainty, they should therefore be willing to lend more and at a better rate. Moreover, these considerations may favour an internationally recognized workout procedure to the extent that they apply to individual transactions as well. In the case of a private investor lending to a foreign country an inefficiency may arise if the borrowing country does not include in the contract a clause addressing the possibilities of default in order not to send the negative signal that default is a likely contingency. As discussed in Aghion and Hermalin (1990), one way to avoid this inefficiency is to provide an institutionalized bankruptcy procedure which applies by default to every individual debt contract.

An internationally recognized bankruptcy procedure could then be seen as one of the many instances in which for one of the parties it is optimal to commit *ex ante* to a specific behaviour. All international capital markets could work more smoothly. An explicit, recognised procedure would reduce uncertainty (unlike the Paris and London Clubs). Lenders would know that there will be negotiations in which specified rules and procedures will be followed, and if the negotiations break down they would know the size of the collateral. Ultimately every bankruptcy procedure has some element of negotiation among parties (the negotiation could happen even before the bankruptcy), but the rules of the procedure affect the way the negotiation is conducted and the stakes to which the parties are entitled in the event of it breaking down. A bankruptcy procedure, if well designed, would guarantee that the entire process would run more smoothly.

Another feature of a bankruptcy procedure that provides protection – and hence *ex-ante* incentives to the creditors to lend at reasonable rates – is the rule that determines the order in which creditors are paid in the event of default, known as the 'absolute priority rule'. This represents a form of protection to the senior creditors against the interests of other creditors. The absolute priority rule guarantees that the seniority of the creditors is respected in allocating the amount of the collateral in the event of a default. One effect of this rule, if respected by a bankruptcy procedure, is to reduce the monitoring costs of creditors. They need not worry about whether the debtor takes on new junior debts since their interest is protected in any event. If the rule is enforced, creditors will be willing to give credit at better conditions, and the credit market will be more liquid and will work better (see Cornelli and Felli, 1994, for a discussion of this point).

The way in which a bankruptcy procedure can commit creditors at the liquidation stage to comply with the absolute priority rule is by specifying a well-defined structure for the negotiation that will eventually occur in the event of default; in other words by requiring a pre-specified procedure enforced by the bankruptcy authority. In this respect the use of unstructured 'Coasian' negotiation may be *ex-ante* inefficient since it may imply a violation of the absolute priority rule. It is easy to construct examples in which the wrong structure (extensive form) of the negotiation may lead to a violation of the absolute priority rule.[4] Furthermore, it is possible to think of situations in which respect of the absolute priority rule will contrast with the *ex-post* efficiency discussed above. In Cornelli and Felli (1994) an example is given in which an extensive form of the negotiation similar to the one imposed by Chapter 11 in the United States creates a situation whereby pursuing *ex-post* efficiency requires a violation of the absolute priority rule in favour of more junior creditors.

3.3   Renegotiation

In general, the incentive to renegotiate the existing terms of the debt contract, although desirable from an *ex-post* efficiency point of view, may have undesirable effects on *ex-ante* efficiency, in particular on the creditors' incentives. It is therefore useful to review some of the problems associated with *ex-post* renegotiation.

When a company is experiencing financial distress, the managers may try to negotiate privately with the creditors in order to solve the problem, whether a bankruptcy procedure is in place or not. Franks and Torous (1989) show that private workouts are quite frequent in the corporate world. It is crucial to realize, however, that even if the parties never enter the bankruptcy procedure their behaviour during the negotiation will be deeply affected by the existence of a bankruptcy procedure. Throughout the bargaining process the parties know that if they do not solve their problems privately the next step will be the bankruptcy procedure, and they are aware of the type of protection they will have in this case. At each stage of the bargaining process, therefore, bankruptcy is the option affecting their bargaining power and thus what they will obtain in the end.

It is useful to remember that in a world of perfect information there is no reason why parties should ever end up in court, with all the extra costs that this entails. They should always be able to settle their problems outside. This does not mean that a bankruptcy law in such a world is irrelevant, since it will determine the way parties will settle out of court. One reason why parties might end up in court is if they have incomplete and asymmetric information. Using the court might be the only way in which the offers the parties make will be acceptable (incentive compatible) (Spier, 1992). These aspects would also be important in the context of sovereign debt; in this case too, financial distress which has not yet reached the point of a major crisis may be solved privately.

A good bankruptcy procedure should provide the right incentives for parties to solve problems right at the start, thus avoiding the problems of loss of confidence and spread of fear that international defaults usually cause. A procedure that favours one party too much (in particular the debtor) would also have the effect of inducing this party to refuse any other agreement and to end up in formal bankruptcy more often than would be optimal. Therefore the fact that parties to the debt contract may renegotiate out of the bankruptcy procedure does not necessarily imply the failure of the *ex-ante* efficiency effects of the procedure itself.

The *ex-ante* efficiency effects of a bankruptcy procedure are reinforced when, as may occur in the sovereign debt context, the phenomenon of financial distress and default is repeated. In a corporate bankruptcy it is difficult to talk about a repeated default, since default tends to be a once and for all event. Indeed, in the corporate context bankruptcy may lead to liquidation which (almost by definition) prevents the firm from finding itself in the same situation again. The repetition of default is more frequent in an international framework since the country remains operating and it is therefore possible to talk about reputation. If reputation helps when there is no collateral, it helps even more when there is collateral. Bernheim and Whinston (1990) show that when firms compete in more than one market it is easier to sustain cooperation in each market, since each firm could be punished simultaneously in many markets. The same conclusion could be reached in the different context of international bankruptcy. Since a country has contacts and relationships with other countries in many fields, and in particular it receives financing in many forms (in part as a country, in part as financing for private firms) it might be easier to enforce an agreement if the other countries agree to 'punish' the defaulting country on other grounds.

Another relevant issue when discussing renegotiation within or outside a bankruptcy procedure is the fact that the higher the number of creditors, the more difficult it is to coordinate the bargaining process. In particular, if there are a large number of creditors for a small amount, there will be a strong externality among the creditors. Every lender has an incentive to free ride on the other lenders and refuse to write down the debt. If some lenders agree to write down the face value of their credit, others may succeed in remaining lenders for the entire amount. This aspect has been underlined by Gertner and Scharfstein (1991), who show that the restructuring of the debt is much easier in the case of bank lending (which usually involves a relatively small number of lenders) than in the case of bondholders.

These problems can only be greater in the case of sovereign debtors. Two solutions are suggested. First, bank credit rather than bond financing might be encouraged. Second, given that in any case sovereign lenders very often use bonds (because of the large amounts they need to borrow), there is an incentive to amend *ex ante* this feature of bond lending in order to make the *ex-post* renegotiation easier. This can be accomplished by requiring bonds to have a clause that makes it easier to convince the lenders to accept a writedown of their debt. For example, less than unanimity might be required in order to accept a writedown for all bonds. Alternatively, the bondholders who agreed to write down part of their debt might in exchange become more senior than the bondholders who did not. Finally, a judicial authority might be introduced in the bankruptcy procedure with the right to impose a writedown on bond-financed debt.

In the context of perfect information creditors should voluntarily arrive at the writedown of credits when it is economically appropriate. Thus the mediation of a judicial authority might not be necessary. This is the principle on which Chapter 11 is based: the creditors should spontaneously agree to writedowns. In reality, however, some creditors may try to hold up the others in order to obtain more. This is why there is a rule in Chapter 11 called 'cramdown'. If some creditors refuse to approve a plan in which they obtain more than what they would obtain in liquidation, the other parties may go to the court and the judge may assign the blocking creditors only the amount they would have obtained in liquidation. It may, however, be rational for creditors to behave in this way in a context of imperfect information. In general, it is not clear how much each party would obtain in liquidation since the liquidation value of the assets is unclear. This may be particularly true in an international context, where it is not clear whether and how a number of assets might be seized. Consider the value of certain public services provided by a country. Even if it seems that a judicial authority might help in this situation (as it does in Chapter 11), it should be remembered that the judicial authority could be the party with the least information of all.

The appropriate bankruptcy procedure should therefore try to encourage the parties to reveal their private information. Letting the parties make proposals is one way of encouraging revelation; another is to tie the terms on which creditors' claims are settled to a binding commitment on their part to inject new funds. By revealing their willingness to inject new funds, creditors are also revealing their expectations about the growth possibilities of the country and therefore their willingness to accept writedowns. On the other hand, it may also be relevant to induce the debtor to reveal its private information. One possibility would be to let the debtor reveal its private information by making proposals. Alternatively, it may be asked to choose from a 'menu' of writedowns and new funds: if it accepts new funds in the amount of 100, creditors will write down 50% of their credits, but if it wants new funds in the amount of 500, then creditors will write down only 20% of their credits. By choosing from the menu a debtor would self-select and in this way reveal its information concerning the value of the project at hand.

It should be noted that using a debtor's offers to induce it to reveal its private information may alter the creditors' *ex-ante* incentives. As we argued above, the structure and order of offers is one of the mechanisms though which certain *ex-ante* efficiency properties of the bankruptcy procedure are implemented. Soliciting offers may create a tension between eliciting private information and preserving, for example, the absolute priority rule (Cornelli and Felli, 1994).

3.4 *Ex-ante* incentives of the debtor

We turn now to the *ex-ante* efficiency considerations associated with the correct incentives of the debtor. This is obtained by means of the threat of loss of the collateral in the event of default and the threat of loss of the job as manager of the debt. In all corporate bankruptcy procedures the judicial authority in charge or the creditors may replace the firm's manager. It is difficult, however, to imagine a procedure that would allow the foreign creditors to impose a new government in the debtor country. Not being able to replace the management is not in principle a bad idea. After all, Chapter 11 uses the 'debtor in possession' clause, under which during the bankruptcy procedure the debtor (or the old management) remains in control of the company. The assumption underlying this rule is that whoever had the control before has the best information about how to run the company and therefore should keep doing it. The judicial authority will replace the management only if it is shown to be incompetent or in bad faith. Conversely, a procedure like receivership in the United Kingdom allows for replacement of the debtor by assuming that a representative of the creditors with the floating charge, once in control of the firm, could easily collect all the necessary information.

We think that in the case of sovereign debt the private information held by the country government and administration is substantial and therefore, even if possible, it would not be optimal to replace the manager of the debt. Requiring the government of the debtor country to discuss its economic plans for the future could suffice. Naturally the case of obviously bad government remains, but this should be decided by the voters of the debtor country. In the sovereign debt environment – as opposed to the corporate environment – if for efficiency reasons the creditors have a say in the government of the debtor country, this would clearly represent a violation of the sovereignty of the debtor country. The voters should have sole control of the government; the voters' incentives to make sure that the government in place keeps the servicing of the foreign debt as a high priority should be indirectly provided though the choice of the correct collateral. Once again a portfolio of private firm bonds might be an ideal way to achieve both goals.

We mentioned above that some of the procedures available in corporate bankruptcy are not feasible in the context of sovereign debt; for example, the case in which the creditors become the new shareholders of the bankrupt firm (Aghion, Hart and Moore, 1992). Something similar could, however, happen in the case of over-extended sovereign debt. Note that once again this case is more easily dealt with if the areas in which the government is over-extended can be connected to the debt. Otherwise the only power the judicial authority has, if any, may be to impose the discussion of an economic plan with the creditors. If, instead, the lending is more explicitly restricted to a particular project then foreign lenders may become equity holders of the assets involved in the project. Countries are usually reluctant to accept foreign ownership, but this could be an advantage: it could be seen as a last resort in case the government does not succeed in restructuring, repaying the debt and reducing its presence. It would therefore be a good incentive for the government to restructure and privatize. Moreover, it must be remembered that the rationale for creditors to become shareholders in bankruptcy theory is that the assets would be in the hands of those who maximize their value. This suggests precisely that the ownership of these assets should change, and it might even go to foreigners. We proposed above the use of shares of private firms of the debtor country as a collateral. If the firms are public, the proposal may still have merits. It could even become a privatization device.

3.5   Improving *ex-ante* contractual arrangements

The credit market can be improved and made smoother not only by imposing *ex-post* rules that guarantee a smooth decision process in case of default. Some restrictions can be imposed *ex ante* on the contracts in which the debtor is allowed to enter. This could have two effects: to avoid default as much as possible and, in case default happens, to guarantee a debt-ownership structure that minimizes the possibility of conflicts among creditors. One way to do this is, as discussed also in Franks (1995), by limiting the capital structure of the government's financing.

One problem associated with this approach, however, is that the maturity structure of the debt may yield violations of the seniority structure. If the junior debt is due before the senior debt, it may be that by the time the senior debt is due no more wealth is left to repay it. The authority in charge of the bankruptcy procedure should therefore monitor the seniority and maturity of the debt issued. This can be done only if the lenders share all the information. In all these cases the problem arises of how to guarantee the commitment of the lenders to provide the correct information and to lend only as allowed. *Ex post*, in fact, a creditor has an incentive to protect its own credit, imposing an externality on the other creditors. One possibility could be to guarantee the creditors protection in case of default – that is guarantee that they will have a part in the orderly workout proceedings as agreed *ex ante* – only if the terms of their lending respect the limits imposed by the authority. Otherwise all their credit (included the part that does respect the limits) will receive only secondary protection. Again, creditors have an incentive to commit *ex ante* to limit their possible actions in order to achieve a better coordination which is in everybody's interest.

4   Final issues

Before concluding two issues deserve more discussion. These are: how to implement a bankruptcy procedure which has the features discussed above; and who should have the right to initiate such a procedure.

In the first issue the question is whether some form of structured bargaining would be more or less desirable than a 'binding arbitration'. The answer seems to lie with the related question of whether a binding arbitration might reproduce the effects of a bankruptcy workout. Given our previous discussion it is clear that in a situation of perfect information the binding arbitration can always reproduce and eventually improve on the outcome of the parties' workout. The arbitrator can always compute what the result of the bankruptcy workout would be and then impose it as a solution. In general, however, in the presence of perfect information arbitration would be better than any other procedure when all the other problems mentioned above arise. Consider, for example, compliance with the absolute priority rule. It is hard to imagine that *ex-post* arbitration, in the absence of some structure imposed on the negotiation among the creditors leading to the workout, would be able to achieve an allocation that complies with this rule.

The analysis extends to the presence of imperfect information. If contracts are complete the same conclusion will be reached. In the presence of imperfect information, bargaining does not in general achieve efficiency. This is because the different parties, in making the offers, will try to withhold information and this could lead, for example, to choosing liquidation, when it would have been better to put additional funds into the project and keep it going. The question is whether the arbitrator would be able to improve on this outcome. A reasonable assumption about the information structure of the arbitrator would be that the arbitrator is uninformed: his information is equivalent to that of the least informed party. This implies that he has to induce the parties to reveal truthfully their private information. The revelation principle, however, guarantees that the framework in which parties reveal their private information and a central authority (the arbitrator) decides the *ex-post* allocation is equivalent to any environment in which parties choose offers or take other strategic decisions that reveal their private information. Thus when contracts are complete, once again the outcome of any privately negotiated workout may be reproduced by an arbitrator. This depends, however, on the arbitrator having the necessary tools to induce the parties to reveal the truth, that is on contracts being complete. When these tools are not available the situation may change, although in general the conclusions might still be true provided that the set of tools available to the arbitrator is the same as the set of contractual tools available to the individual parties. In this case some constrained form of the revelation principle might still apply and in general the arbitrator might be able to reproduce the decentralized allocation (Tirole, 1994).

A final consideration should be the choice of the arbitrator. The above discussion relies heavily on the arbitrator being fully rational and a 'benevolent central planner'. In the absence of these characteristics a number of problems may arise. The arbitrator might be biased towards the debtor and against the creditors or *vice versa*. In general, it is possible to envisage situations in which the arbitrator is pursuing a personal agenda that differs from the efficient allocation described above. This clearly requires either a very careful choice of arbitrator or a procedure that more closely uses the existing market mechanisms. We think that the suggested choice of the collateral as a set of private firm bonds might be an appropriate tool.

The second issue concerns who initiates a workout procedure. Typically, in a corporate bankruptcy procedure only the debtor has the right to declare bankruptcy and initiate the procedure. Lenders, however, often include 'cross-default' clauses in their contracts stating that if the debtor defaults with any other lender then it is automatically defaulting with them too, even if the repayment of their debt is not yet due. This is of course to protect creditors. In this context it is clear that it is enough to give only the debtor the ability to initiate a bankruptcy procedure. If the debtor has to default with one creditor, it is going to default with all the other creditors. It may then choose to apply for the bankruptcy procedure in order to get the 'automatic stay' (that is in order to avoid the grabbing of assets by the creditors). Note, however, that this modifies the rules of the private workouts. Imagine that a firm is in financial distress but has not yet defaulted. It might begin private workouts with its creditors in order to restructure its debts. This could be modelled as bargaining in which the debtor has an outside option (declaring bankruptcy) but the creditors do not (at least not until the date for the repayment arrives). Changing this rule means modifying the outside option of the parties involved in the bargaining and eventually arriving at violations of the absolute priority rule.

All this has to be taken into account when choosing a rule in an international context. In this case, however, an additional problem arises. Assume again that only the debtor has the right to declare bankruptcy. Because of the sovereignty of the debtor, however, creditors have less chance to grab the assets and therefore there is less pressure on the debtor to declare bankruptcy at the right time. The problem in this case is that a debtor always has an incentive to delay declaring bankruptcy in the hope that in the meantime things might get better (Myers, 1977). But if bankruptcy is declared later than it should be, assets could lose value in the meantime. This seems to imply that creditors or a general body should also have the power to initiate a bankruptcy procedure. Here the issue of asymmetry of information would become relevant. Before the actual default the debtor is the only one able to assess its ability to repay its debts. Any interference from other parties would only make things worse. It might therefore be better to leave the right to declare bankruptcy to the debtor alone with some additional rule about the acceleration of other debts in case of one default.

Notes

1. Assessing the values of the claims is usually one of the most time-consuming tasks of any bankruptcy procedure.

2. Note that throughout our discussion we use the term collateral to identify the set of assets all the creditors can appropriate in the event of default. As discussed below the presence of the collateral is critical in identifying the role and the benefits of a bankruptcy procedure. There is, however, an alternative meaning for the term collateral that refers to a specific asset which serves as guarantee for an individual debt. Clearly, the availability of collateral so interpreted is less crucial, although it may help in determining the benefits of a bankruptcy procedure.

3. Also Franks (1995) suggests a similar approach to improve the collateralization of debt.

4. Consider, for example, a bankruptcy procedure that in line with Chapter 11 allows only the debtor to make a restructuring proposal in the first few periods after the bankruptcy procedure is initiated. If time is costly this would imply a non-trivial bargaining power of the debtor that may lead to leaving part of the collateral in the hands of the debtor even though the absolute priority rule would require the entire collateral to be distributed in the required order to the foreign investors.

References

Aghion, P., Hart, O. and Moore, J. (1992), 'The Economics of Bankruptcy Reform', *Journal of Law, Economics and Organizations* 8, pp. 523–546.

Aghion, P. and Hermalin, B. (1990), 'Legal Restrictions on Private Contracts Can Enhance Efficiency', *Journal of Law, Economics and Organizations* 6, pp. 381–409.

Baird, D. and Picker, R.C. (1991), 'A Simple Non-cooperative Bargaining Model of Corporate Reorganizations', *Journal of Legal Studies* 20, pp. 311–349.

Bernheim, M. and Whinston, D.B. (1990), 'Multimarket Contact and Collusive Behavior', *RAND Journal of Economics* 21, pp. 1–26.

Cornelli, F. and Felli, L. (1994), 'Efficiency of Bankruptcy Procedures', Bank of Italy Working paper No. 245.

Cornelli, F. and Li, D. (1994), 'Large Shareholders, Control Benefits and Optimal Schemes for Privatization', CEPR Discussion Paper No. 891.

Eaton, J. and Fernandez, R. (1994), 'Sovereign Debt', in *Handbook of International Economics*, A.G. Atkenson and T. Persson (eds.), forthcoming.

Franks, J. R. (1995), 'Some Issues in Sovereign Debt and Distressed Reorganizations', this volume.

Franks, J.R. and Torous, W.N. (1989), 'An Empirical Investigation of US Firms in Chapter 11 Reorganizations', *Journal of Finance* 44, pp. 747–67.

Gertner, R. and Scharfstein, D. (1991), 'A Theory of Workouts and the Effects of Reorganization Law', *Journal of Finance* 46, pp. 1189–1222.

Myers, S.C. (1977), 'Determinants of Corporate Borrowing', *Journal of Financial Economics* 5, pp. 147–75.

Spier, K.E. (1992), 'The Dynamics of Pretrial Bargaining', *Review of Economic Studies* 59, pp. 93–108.

Tirole, J. (1994), 'Incomplete Contracts: Where Do We Stand?', Walras-Bowley lecture delivered at the 1994 North American Summer Meetings of the Econometric Society, Quebec City.

Annex 2

Some issues in sovereign debt and distressed reorganizations

Julian Franks
London Business School and CEPR

1   Introduction

In sovereign debt contracts there has been historically a lack of willingness to accept formally the possibility of default, and this has made it difficult to define the process of reorganization in the event of default. The evidence on interest rates paid by sovereign borrowers suggests that lenders have not charged lower interest rates as a result of this uncertainty. A study by the Federal Reserve Bank of New York found that most sovereign debt carried higher yields than similarly rated corporate debt.[1] Also when default has occurred governments have been compelled not only to reschedule debt, and thereby implicitly reduce its value, but also to make drastic writedowns in face values. For example, in September 1995 the Nicaraguan government made a formal offer to commercial creditors to buy back $1.3 billion of recognised commercial debt for a maximum of 8 cents in the dollar.

In contrast, the process for resolving a corporate default is subject to far less uncertainty. For example, the United Kingdom's receivership code and the United States's Chapter 11 provide well defined processes of reorganization.[2]

Two issues are examined in this paper. First, some of the problems in carrying over the principles of corporate bankruptcy to sovereign debt reorganization are described. For example, in corporate reorganization the value of the assets is either known because the assets have been sold, or new securities can be given to creditors in the reorganized company thereby mitigating some of the valuation problems (see Bebchuk, 1988; and Aghion, Hart and Moore, 1992). As a result, it is relatively easy to accommodate writedowns that reflect the fall in the value of the firm. In contrast, there is no obvious metric for valuing a country's assets (i.e. the analogue to the value of the firm), so determining the size of the cake to be divided among creditors and the size of any writedowns is a daunting task.

Second, some proposals for improving the contractual arrangements for sovereign borrowing are discussed. The objectives of such arrangements are threefold: to clarify the property rights of lenders in the event of default; to improve the capital structure of a sovereign state's financing; and to lower the interest rates paid by sovereign borrowers.

2   Application of the main features of US and UK corporate bankruptcy codes for sovereign state reorganization

Some of the main features of Chapter 11 of the US Bankruptcy code and receivership of the UK code and the potential for transferring them to a reorganization code for a sovereign state are described below. The existing and new German codes are also referred to briefly.[3]

2.1   The United States's Chapter 11

2.1.1   Judicial authority as umpire

A judicial authority acts as umpire and supervises the reorganization process to ensure it accords with the law. It is a very active process, and the debtor in possession must report to the judicial authority on a continuing basis and obtain permission for any substantial actions such as major sales and investments. The creditors are frequently consulted before the judicial decision.

The equivalent authority could be something like the European Court. The advantage of a judicial authority is that it would be less prone to political judgements. This is important because if creditors see the process as a political one, they will impose a risk premium in lending rates. But it is difficult to contemplate carrying over the continuing process of consultations and permissions that is one of the hallmarks of the Chapter 11 process.

2.1.2   Automatic stay

Automatic stay provisions postpone the payment of interest and principal on most debts so as to avoid disrupting the company's activities. This is to avoid the main market failure, which is the race by creditors to grab assets. It also allows the firm to continue trading provided it has positive operating cash flow.

This is one of the most important principles incorporated into many bankruptcy codes. A three-month mandatory moratorium has just been incorporated into the new German code (passed in 1994). In the UK administration procedure there is an automatic stay for three months which can be renewed only with creditor agreement. The UK government has just proposed a one-month moratorium (with important qualifications) for the UK receivership code. An important difference between the US code and the UK (and new German) codes is that the judge has wide discretion to extend automatic stay in Chapter 11, whereas the UK code either allows a stay only with creditors' permission or limits the length of the stay to, say, three months.

It would not be difficult in principle to provide for an automatic stay for sovereign debt. Such a clause could be made part of the bond contract or agreed by the principal lenders, or it could be part of an international agreement. In practice, states have imposed an automatic stay by simply refusing to pay and, in the absence of an enforcement mechanism, creditors have been forced to accept such stays. This is unsatisfactory, however, since such unregulated stays cannot be *ex-ante* efficient and must be paid for in higher interest rates.[4]

2.1.3 Debtor in possession

In the first instance, the defaulting company, called the debtor in possession, remains in control of the company. The judge in bankruptcy can change the management, however, for example at the request of the creditors. The experience with Chapter 11 cases is that in about 50% of cases new management is appointed before the firm emerges from reorganization.[5]

This opportunity to change management would be difficult to apply to a country and is politically unacceptable. As we shall discuss below, however, transferring state borrowing to agencies or companies makes this possibility much more viable. A modified objective would be provisions that allow the international authority to impose conditions on the management of the state's financial affairs, as the IMF does today. But there remains a serious problem of enforcement.

2.1.4 Creditors are entitled to the value of the firm according to absolute priority

After default, the creditors are entitled to the proceeds of the sale of the company or securities that have rights to the assets. Although in principle strict absolute priority is the rule, that is senior creditors' claims must be satisfied before more junior claims (including equity) may receive any of the proceeds, the reality is different. There is strong evidence of deviations from absolute priority both in Chapter 11 reorganizations and in distressed exchanges (often referred to as workouts). One recent study reports deviations from absolute priority of 9.51% in favour of equityholders in distressed exchanges and 2.28% in Chapter 11 reorganizations. Bank and senior debt make the largest contributions (see Franks and Torous, 1994; and Weiss, 1990).

The process of agreeing writedowns is especially difficult in sovereign bankruptcy because there is no simple analogue to the value of the firm. As a result, it is difficult to agree the size of any writedowns to the debt outstanding. Metrics could be developed to capture a country's capacity to service its debt, for example, the GNP of a country or the value of its foreign trade. This has historically been made more difficult by the need for unanimity (or near unanimity) among members of lending consortia negotiating with the defaulting state.

The valuation problem has also been made more complex in the past by disagreements on the priority of claims. For example, the difference between secured and unsecured claims in sovereign debt has often not been recognized. In the inter-war period the US government refused to agree to plans that offered larger payouts to secured debt held by UK holders (see Eichengreen and Portes, 1990).

2.1.5 Supra-priority finance

Chapter 11 allows the insolvent firm to raise new financing which is senior to most existing financing subject to the agreement of the court. Such financing does not in principle impair the collateral of the claims of secured debt. It will, however, dilute the claims of unsecured or partially secured claims.

Supra-priority financing is especially important in Chapter 11 since firms may remain in Chapter 11 for a considerable period of time. In one sample, the average period spent in

Chapter 11 was more than two years (see Franks and Torous, 1994). An extreme example often cited to illustrate the abuse of supra-priority financing is that of Eastern Airlines, which entered Chapter 11 in the Southern District of New York. It had sufficient funds when it entered of $3.7 billion to repay debts of $3.4 billion. When the firm was eventually liquidated the creditors received only $0.34 billion. Much of the loss in value was attributed to the ease with which the company was able to raise supra-priority financing to pay for operating losses.

The problem is very different for sovereign debt since the covenants rarely include a requirement that limits a country's borrowing. As a result, states can raise supra-priority financing without the agreement of creditors, thereby effectively diluting existing claims. Even where the international capital markets are closed to the borrower, the state can raise new loans through trade credit or through special agreements involving payment in kind. Only where the borrowing is secured will the creditor have some form of protection, although this may be limited as we discuss below.

2.1.6 Non-unanimity provisions

There are important non-unanimity provisions regarding the approval of the plan of reorganization. The main provision is that the plan requires a majority of creditors by number and two-thirds by value in all classes of creditors. Such provisions significantly mitigate creditor holdout and free-rider problems.[6]

The importance of these provisions is illustrated by the growth in pre-packaged Chapter 11s, where the principal creditors agree a plan of reorganization and then enter Chapter 11 so that the plan can be put to creditors using these non-unanimity provisions.[7] Pre-packaged Chapter 11s accounted for 43% of filings in the first six months of 1993 for firms with assets greater than $100 million.

In contrast, in sovereign defaults, unanimity (or near unanimity) has often been a serious constraint if not a requirement to obtain approval of a plan.

2.1.7 Financing the reorganization

A variety of new instruments can be given in exchange for existing claims including equity for debt swaps. This is absolutely vital in both workouts and formal reorganization plans approved in Chapter 11. The creditors are frequently offered new equity securities or warrants in exchange for old debt.[8]

The instruments given in sovereign bankruptcy are usually more limited since equity cannot be given unless the loan is for project financing. Without new equity or quasi-equity, the state is denied an important mechanism for rectifying an inappropriate capital structure.

2.2   The United Kingdom's receivership code

Whereas control rights are largely given to the debtor in possession in Chapter 11, in the UK code they are given to creditors. The principal code, other than liquidation, is receivership which gives virtually all control rights to a particular secured creditor (the creditor holding a floating charge on the company's assets).

A change in control is triggered by a default defined by the provisions of the debt contract. The court need not be involved in the appointment of the receiver, unless the company argues that default has not been triggered.[9] The creditor holding the floating charge appoints a receiver who may, subject to some qualifications, manage the company with the sole objective of realizing sufficient proceeds to repay the appointer's claims. It is an often quoted phrase that 'the receiver is king'. US companies, accustomed to Chapter 11, find it difficult to comprehend fully the highly creditor-oriented nature of the UK code.

Since control rights in receivership are given to secured creditors, the rights of unsecured creditors are very limited. It is often the case that unsecured creditors are not aware that a receiver is liquidating the company until it has already happened.

Clearly the applicability of the UK code to sovereign default is limited. The main idea is that control rights are given to secured lenders, i.e. loans are collateralized, and that where default takes place the creditor should be entitled to the asset or the revenue from the asset that it has a lien on. Carrying over the UK code to sovereign default, however, would involve a clear definition of the property rights of the lender and low-cost enforcement mechanisms. It would also require an important secured creditor. As discussed below, such issues are complex and controversial.

The comparison of the UK receivership code and the US Chapter 11 also suggests the potential for differences of view among member governments as to what constitutes an efficient bankruptcy code.[10]

2.3   Competing jurisdictions

Where assets in one country are owned by shareholders in another, a problem of competing jurisdictions can arise in the bankruptcy process. Such an issue arose in the Maxwell case when the UK company was placed in administration and the US company entered Chapter 11. The administrator appointed by the UK court wished to manage the US company while it was in Chapter 11, against the wishes of the US management. In this case, the administrator would have been responsible to two legal authorities which would not necessarily agree on the disposition of the US company's assets. In the event, the US judge agreed to allow the administrator to manage the US company, but on condition that a trustee was appointed by the court to oversee the administrator's actions. As discussed below, in the EU, laws agreed to by member governments regulate both the jurisdiction of a commercial case and the particular country's law (they may be different in the two cases).

2.4   Summary

Any discussion of the application of corporate bankruptcy to international bankruptcy laws should appreciate the lack of unanimity both within and across countries about what is the correct model to apply. For example, there is serious criticism of Chapter 11 in the United States. It is regarded as very costly, and the wide discretion given to *ex-post* changes in debt contracts is regarded by some as being *ex-ante* inefficient.[11] Recent changes to the code in 1994 have made only modest improvements. Similarly, the UK receivership code has been seriously criticized for providing too little incentive to retain businesses as going concerns.[12] As a result, the UK government is currently considering changes to the law.

There are nevertheless some common themes running through many bankruptcy codes. The concept of at least a limited standstill on debts commands wide support. It is an important element in the new German code which is due to come into force in 1999, and it has been proposed in a consultation paper issued by the UK government. The important questions are the length of such a stay and what provisions there should be to prevent the debtor selling assets or raising new funds which dilute existing creditors' rights.

A second theme is that the rights of secured lenders should be safeguarded. This is an important element of both the UK and US codes. It is difficult to see how debt markets could function efficiently without such safeguards. This marks an important difference in sovereign debt markets where secured lending is less common and it may be far more difficult in some countries to enforce claims when default occurs. A point made below is that sovereign debt markets could be improved if property rights relating to collateral could be made more transparent and enforcement less costly. This would improve not only *ex-post* efficiency but also *ex-ante* contracting, with important implications for the pricing of sovereign debt.[13]

3   Contractual arrangements in sovereign financing

One way of improving sovereign debt markets is to make sovereign lending more efficient. Improved bankruptcy procedures can contribute by making *ex-post* recontracting less costly. A second route is to improve contractual arrangements for sovereign lending. In reality these two approaches both rely on well-defined property rights and an enforcement mechanism in the debtor country and in third-party countries if the debtor's assets are held overseas.

Five ideas for improving sovereign debt markets are considered below:

- Greater clarity concerning the property rights of creditors and their enforcement.

- Dispersal of sovereign debt to (quasi) corporate entities without cross-guarantees.

- Improved collateralization of debt.

- Widening of financial instruments to improve risk sharing.

- Limiting the capital structure of the government's financing.

An important question in considering the need for intervention in any of these contractual arrangements is why private debt markets have not evolved, or cannot evolve, to deal with these contractual problems (see Sussman, 1994). Some evidence is provided showing that there are serious impediments to enforcing particular debt contractual arrangements. These impediments relate, for example, to the enforcement of collateral provisions in secured loans, and to the lack of well-defined property rights in many countries which make enforcement of claims difficult.

3.1 Clarity of property rights and their enforcement

Chapter 9 of the US code, which governs the bankruptcy of public/political bodies, expressly forbids the courts to interfere in the political powers of public bodies, the debtor's property or revenue, and the use of the income from property. It is interesting to contrast this provision with laws governing the default of UK local authorities, which allow creditors rights to particular revenues of the authority. The UK courts, however, have the power to declare certain transactions *ultra vires* and therefore to relieve (partially or fully) local authorities of their debts, as illustrated in the House of Lords judgment in the Hammersmith and Fulham swaps case.

Legislation in the United Kingdom and in the European Union has clarified the immunity of states which engage in commercial transactions.[14] For example, in the case of Phillip Brothers v. Republic of Sierre Leone and Others, the UK courts permitted a creditor to enforce its rights in a debt contract against the bank accounts and other assets of the foreign state in the United Kingdom. Furthermore, the rights were also enforced against the debtor's assets in France. In this particular case, however, the state waived its immunity rights in the debt contract.

Discussions with practitioners have suggested important limitations to enforcement of collateral. For example, debtor states can thwart the enforcement of such contracts by transferring the title of assets which are to be exported to third parties before they leave the debtor's country. Thus the debtor could in principle sell oil to a third party in its own country prior to export, thereby providing bills of lading showing possession by the third party rather than by the debtor. This makes it difficult or impossible to obtain permission from the court in a third country to seize the goods. The creditor could only prevent this change of ownership if property rights were so defined in the debtor country that its own or foreign courts could determine that such transfers of title were invalid according to the debtor country's laws.[15]

There are several possible changes which may improve sovereign debt contracts. Individual countries could alter their laws to give greater clarity to property rights of lenders of sovereign debt. As in the United Kingdom, they may have to pass laws waiving immunity in particular cases such as commercial transactions. Also individual countries could sign up to a treaty clarifying which national courts have jurisdiction and which national laws should be applied in particular cases. Such legislation has been passed by member states in the EU. Finally, an international enforcement mechanism is set up to enforce these rights. It is relevant here that most countries in the EU have agreed to abide by decisions of the European Court, even though there is no enforcement mechanism.

3.2   Dispersal of country debt without cross-guarantees

Governments frequently permit some activities of a state or local government to be financed by private debt markets without a guarantee by central government. For example, the debts of US city or state governments are not guaranteed by the Federal government. As a result, the bankruptcy of New York City or Orange County should not directly affect the solvency of other institutions.[16] Similarly, the debts of local authorities in the United Kingdom are not guaranteed by the central government.[17]

The concept of relating the public debt of a country to particular revenue streams and managerial activities, without central government guarantee, has three advantages. First, it allows the dispersal of debt thereby enforcing greater discipline on government financing. It can therefore advance the diversification of managerial failure. Thus those who manage the activities appreciate that default may impair their jobs and the jobs of those for whom they are responsible. Second, it reduces systemic risks since the default of one part of government activities does not affect another. Third, lenders will be compelled to monitor these activities to ensure that repayment can be made, and such a service may add value not only to lenders but also to sovereign borrowers.

The devolution of borrowing can only be accomplished where the borrowing is raised on assets or income that can service the debt. Trading or manufacturing companies owned or partially owned by the state or institutions that have tax-raising powers would readily fit into this category. Selling part or all of the shares in state companies can provide an important mechanism for detaching central government guarantees from activities previously administered by government. A sale of shares, however, may not necessarily be a prerequisite. The state-owned Israel Electric Corporation has recently agreed with the government to raise debt on the basis of its own credit rating. It intends to raise $600–700 million during the period 1995–2002. This marks the first time that an Israeli state company has gone to the international debt markets without government guarantee (see *Financial Times*, 17 August 1995).

There are a number of potential disadvantages to such a policy. First, some debts could not be allocated with ease to revenue or managerial activities. There would still be debts that would have to be financed out of general revenue. Second, the failure to provide cross-guarantees may increase the interest rate on the debt.[18] Such increases, however, will in part reflect the fact that the debt of one activity does not co-insure the debt of another and therefore the higher interest rate will reflect the higher risks taken by the lender; as a result the borrowing will not prove more costly. Third, there will be a need to monitor these decentralized activities, and in a developing economy this may prove costly and fraught with managerial problems. Such monitoring, however, would be required of the creditor, and it is not obvious that the monitoring would be more expensively done by outside agents of creditors than by the government.

3.3   Improved collateralization of debt

One of the most important differences between sovereign borrowing and corporate borrowing is the proportion of secured debt that is issued. In the United Kingdom, the receivership code can operate only if there is a secured creditor. In Germany Gessner *et al* (1978) reported that 87% of claims against a sample of firms were secured claims. If financial leases are included, security is also important in US lending. Thus the limited amount of such lending to sovereign states must make an important difference to the amount that can be borrowed by some countries and the interest rate charged.

During the inter-war period there were significant problems with creditors trying to gain greater priority of claims on secured debt compared with unsecured debt. The rationale was that if the creditor could not obtain possession of the assets, it did not deserve a prior claim to unsecured creditors.

The ability to collateralize a loan is crucially dependent upon clarity in property rights and the ability to enforce a lien, as discussed earlier.

3.4   Widening of financial instruments to improve risk sharing

Imagine a country whose main source of income is the exploitation of a single asset such as a mineral, and that the price of that asset is highly volatile. What sort of capital structure would you advise for such a country? It would seem most odd and even foolish to advise it to borrow. Indeed it would probably be almost as foolish to suggest that it should finance all the costs with its own equity. The obvious route would be a risk-sharing arrangement whereby another country or corporation took a large slice of the risk in return for part of the revenue. The International Finance Corporation (IFC) has in the past encouraged investors to invest equity in developing countries by offering insurance against very large losses. It made available put options to investors to enable them to limit their downside risk on individual projects; however, the market did not take off because the options were wildly overpriced by the IFC.

Given the default of a large number of very poor countries, with income from highly volatile assets, a debt for equity swap would be an obvious solution. It is an old chestnut yet little is known about why new instruments have not evolved to meet this problem.

3.5   Limiting the capital structure of the government's financing

Companies have limited liability; individuals are liable for their own debts, but not for those of their parents. Contrast this to countries which often borrow on behalf of future generations. Lenders care little whether current or future generations bear the cost of these debts. Defaults have taken place, not as a result of business failure but because of profligacy or lack of political will on the part of the government of the day. We might argue that just as countries need an independent central bank, so they need a policy that commits them in advance to limit their debt.

One obvious solution is for a country to agree to a cap on its borrowing, for example, a maximum ratio of debt (foreign or total) to GNP. This has already been incorporated into the Maastricht Treaty.

Even if we could agree on such a cap, what would happen if the country breached it? One answer would be that countries would prohibit their institutions from lending to it. An alternative is to relate the interest rate in the debt contract to the level of debt outstanding.[19]

4   Conclusion

There are serious problems in translating a corporate bankruptcy code, such as Chapter 11, into a code for sovereign states. It is not simply a matter of which party has the control rights, although that is a formidable problem. There are, in addition, technical issues such as the lack of an obvious metric for valuing the underlying assets of a country which could reasonably be used to repay borrowings. Without such a metric it is difficult to establish the size of the cake to be divided among creditors, and therefore the size of any writedowns.

There is one issue that can be remedied, however, and that is greater clarity in the property rights of creditors. It is unlikely that the uncertainty generated by the lack of clarity and the uncertainty of enforcement is to the advantage of borrowers. Clarification of these issues would not only reduce uncertainty, but may also widen the range of instruments available to sovereign states. Greater secured borrowing would probably result, but that need not be the only opportunity.

Notes

Discussions with Professor Fletcher and several lawyers and insurers were of great value in writing this paper. I am also grateful to Richard Portes and Barry Eichengreen for their comments and suggestions. All errors are my responsibility.

1. Moody's places Argentina's foreign currency debt four notches below investment grade debt.

2. A well-defined process may still be expensive. For example, there has been much criticism of Chapter 11 because of the length of time spent in reorganization and the expense entailed by the debtor firm. Perhaps because of that, however, less costly processes have evolved, for example, pre-packaged Chapter 11s (see text).

3. The description of the three codes draws heavily from Franks and Torous (1994) and Franks, Nyborg and Torous (1995).

4. One reason for *ex-ante* inefficiency is adverse selection.

5. Gilson (1989) reports that management changes are often initiated by creditors, especially bank lenders. Judges may appoint a trustee if they believe that there is evidence of pre-bankruptcy fraud or dishonesty.

6. If one class of creditors votes against a plan the judge may allow that class of creditors to be crammed down; that is they are given the value of the claim based on the liquidation value of the company according to absolute priority. The threat of cramdown is important when there is only one dissenting class.

7. Another reason for obtaining court approval is that it prevents future lawsuits.

8. Gilson (1994), however, has noted that senior debt often refuses to accept significant amounts of new equity in exchange for its debt and as a result the capital structures of firms emerging from reorganization are very heavily burdened with debt. This may explain why a significant proportion of these firms default and re-enter the bankruptcy process.

9. In some circumstances the court can appoint a receiver.

10. For a detailed comparison of the bankruptcy codes of the United States, the United Kingdom and Germany see Franks, Nyborg and Torous (1995).

11. See Baird (1995) for a recent survey.

12. Administration, an alternative code to receivership, can under certain circumstances provide incentives to keep the firm as a going concern (see Franks and Nyborg, 1995).

13. One of the disadvantages of the old German bankruptcy process, however, was that strong rights were given to lenders and they were able to obstruct the sale of the business as a going concern. The old German code remains in force until 1999. Because of the important rights given to secured lenders and their ability to thwart the bankruptcy process, the last two decades have seen a drastic increase in secured lending with a consequent decline in the proportion of companies that can resort to the bankruptcy process as a way of preserving the company as a going concern (see Franks, Nyborg and Torous, 1994).

14. For example, in the United Kingdom the State Immunity Act, 1978.

15. There may be other obstacles to litigation against a state. In some countries, for example, it is necessary to obtain permission from the chief legal officer to sue the state.

16. It may be, however, that if the state's debts are foreign denominated a claim on US foreign exchange reserves increases the risk to other US foreign exchange denominated debt.

17. It should be said, however, that in the 1980s some governments were forced to repay debt of state companies that they had not guaranteed.

18. This is not necessarily the case if such devolution leads to greater efficiency.

19. One problem with such a solution is that the higher interest rate may hasten default.

References

Aghion, P., Hart, O. and Moore, J. (1992), 'The economics of bankruptcy reform', *Journal of Law, Economics & Organization* 8, p. 523–46.

Baird, D. (1995), 'The hidden virtues of Chapter 11: An overview of the Law and economics of financially distressed firms', unpublished paper presented to the Nobel conference on law and economics, Stockholm.

Bebchuk, l. (1988), 'A new approach to corporate reorganization', *Harvard Law Review* 101, p. 775.

Eichengreen, B. and Portes, R. (1990), 'The inter-war debt crisis and its aftermath', *The World Bank Research Observer* 5.1, pp. 69–94.

Franks, J. R., Nyborg, K. and Torous, W. (1995), 'A comparison of US, UK and German insolvency codes', World Bank Working Paper.

Franks, J. R., and Nyborg, K. (1994), 'Control rights and the loss of private benefits: The case of the UK insolvency code', CEPR/ESF Working Paper No. 47.

Franks, J. R., and Torous, W. (1994), 'How shareholders and creditors fare in workouts and Chapter 11 reorganizations', *Journal of Financial Economics*, May.

Gessner, V., Rhode, B., Strate, G. and Ziegert, K. (1978), *Die Praxis der Konkursabwicklung in der Bundesrepublik Deutschland*, Koln, Bundesanzeiger Verlagsges. mbH..

Gilson, S. (1989), 'Management turnover and financial distress', *Journal of Financial Economics* 25, pp. 241–62.

Gilson, S. (1994), 'Capital structure changes in Chapter 11 reorganizations', unpublished manuscript, Harvard Business School.

Sussman, O. (1994), 'Talking about growth: the evolution of contractual language', unpublished manuscript, University of Jerusalem.

Weiss, L. (1990), 'Bankruptcy resolution: direct costs and violation of absolute priority', *Journal of Financial Economics* 27, pp. 285–314.

Annex 3

Considerations of international law

Christopher Greenwood
Magdalene College, Cambridge,
and Essex Court Chambers

Hugh Mercer
Essex Court Chambers

1   Introduction

The purpose of this memorandum is to examine a number of questions of international law arising out of attempts to draw an analogy between bankruptcy proceedings in domestic law and arrangements for the orderly workout of sovereign debt. Three principal questions have to be considered:

- What are the differences in the present legal positions of the main classes of a state's creditors?

- Is there an analogy between the position in international law when a state debtor defaults and the position of a corporation under domestic bankruptcy law?

- Could such an analogy be created (or strengthened)? In particular:

(a) Could a mechanism be devised whereby a restructuring package could be imposed upon dissenting creditors?

(b) To what extent can an individual 'dissenting creditor' be excluded from recourse to the courts when a restructuring plan has been agreed by a majority of creditors?

(c) Is there an international body which could exercise a supervisory role comparable to that of a national court in bankruptcy proceedings?

2   The differences in the present legal positions of the main classes of a state's creditors

States tend to have a wide variety of creditors which can be classed in many different ways. For present purposes, however, the four main classes are other states, international institutions (such as the IMF and the World Bank), foreign private creditors and domestic private creditors. Irrespective of the ways in which loan transactions are structured, there are marked differences between the legal positions of these four classes.

When one state makes a loan to another state, the loan agreement – if it takes a legally binding form – will generally be an international treaty, governed by public international law. Breach of the terms of that treaty will be a violation of international law which will give rise to the same remedies as other such violations. The creditor state may have recourse to the International Court of Justice (if there is a clause in the loan agreement providing for the jurisdiction of this court or if there is some other agreement in force between the creditor and debtor states which would provide a basis for the court's jurisdiction) or to other methods of dispute settlement, such as arbitration, for which there is provision between the parties. It may also take retaliatory action within certain strictly defined limits (for example, freezing assets of the debtor state located in the creditor state's territory) or rely on diplomatic and political pressure. A creditor state would not normally be able to bring an action against a debtor state in a national court. Negotiations between a debtor state and a syndicate of its state creditors (as in the Paris Club) are common, but there is usually no legal obligation on an individual creditor state to participate in such negotiations or to accede to any negotiated solution, so that even if there are successful negotiations, they must be followed by the conclusion of bilateral agreements between the debtor state and each of its creditor states.

International institutions can conclude agreements either under international law or under the law of a particular state. Although they cannot bring proceedings in the International Court of Justice, they frequently have access to other international methods for the settlement of disputes. Provision for arbitration, for example, is common. Since the institutions largely control a debtor state's access to new funds, they frequently have a strong enough negotiating position not to need recourse to a court or other tribunal.

Agreements between a state and its foreign private creditors are almost always subject to a specified system of national law ('the proper law of the contract'), not international law. At one time it was common for a state borrowing money to insist that its own law should be the proper law of the contracts it concluded (see the decision of the Permanent Court of International Justice in the *Case concerning certain Serbian and Brazilian Loans*), but in recent years it has been far more common for creditors to insist that the proper law should be that of the creditor's state or a third country (usually a major financial centre) and to make provision for the courts of that country to be given jurisdiction in the event of a dispute. Private creditors do not have direct access to the International Court of Justice (which can only hear cases between states or give advisory opinions at the request of United Nations bodies) or other international tribunals, but can request their states to take up a case on their behalf in exercise of the right of diplomatic protection. Although such cases have been brought, it is more common for a private creditor to commence an action in the national courts which the loan agreement provides should have jurisdiction or of the state in which the loan was to be repaid. The debtor state will not normally be able to rely on sovereign immunity to prevent such proceedings since the laws in the countries where those proceedings are most frequently brought (United States, United Kingdom, Germany) treat loan and other financial instruments as commercial transactions in respect of which a state is not immune. In any event it is common to include a waiver of immunity in loan agreements.

Domestic private creditors are often in the weakest position. If they bring proceedings in the courts of the debtor state, they are likely to be defeated by the moratorium legislation which that state has adopted. They may bring proceedings in the courts of another state, but in this case they are more likely than foreign creditors to encounter the argument that the courts of the debtor state are a more appropriate forum. There is obviously no state which can represent their interests in dealings with the debtor state.

The result is that if a debtor state defaults on a wide range of its debt repayments, the legal position will be confused by the fact that the various debt instruments will be governed by different systems of law and there will be no one court system which can assert jurisdiction in respect of all the actions which might be brought by creditors.

3   Is there an analogy between the position in international law when a state debtor defaults and that of a corporation under domestic bankruptcy law?

Although a number of systems for the orderly workout of sovereign debt have emerged which resemble aspects of the bankruptcy arrangements under national law (for example, under Chapter 9 or Chapter 11 of the US Code), the essential features of domestic bankruptcy law are absent from international law. It is not simply that there is no institution of state bankruptcy as such or even that there is no prospect of subjecting a defaulting state to the more extreme measures imposed on a bankrupt corporation, such as the appointment of a receiver to take over administration of the corporation from its existing management, or the large-scale sale of assets. A system broadly analogous to bankruptcy could be envisaged which did not go that far. It is rather that there is no court system which can exercise jurisdiction over the totality of a debtor state's obligations and thus impose an orderly workout. International tribunals have no bankruptcy jurisdiction. National courts in states other than the debtor itself may be confronted with claims by private creditors (particularly foreign private creditors) but are very unlikely to have jurisdiction over the claims of creditor states or international institutions. Even in the case of private creditors, a national court will not normally have any coercive powers to require a creditor to accept part payment, since the court will not be able to apply the provisions of its bankruptcy laws to a default by a foreign state. In this respect, a debtor state, though it may be held liable under a debt instrument by a court in the United States or the United Kingdom, is denied a form of protection available to private debtors appearing before those courts.

The result is that although the IMF (or another international body) may advise the debtor state on putting together a package in which the state's creditors were offered only a portion of the interest or capital to which their debt instruments entitled them, there is no means by which those creditors can be compelled by law to accept that package in the way that creditors of a bankrupt corporation can be compelled to accept such a solution.[1] The *Allied Bank* litigation in the United States[2] shows that a national court will not necessarily give effect to a resettlement package when faced with an action by a dissenting private creditor (although the courts in other states might take a different view from that of the Court of Appeals in this case). No court or other body has the authority to impose a settlement on a state creditor.

On the other hand, some of the problems which bankruptcy law is designed to avoid are largely absent in cases of state default. In particular, there is no risk of premature liquidation or need to ensure that the debtor remains in possession, and access to the debtor state's assets is difficult. In contrast to the position of a private company, all of whose assets will usually be available to creditors, for several reasons only a very small proportion of a state's assets will be available for execution. Most of the state's assets will be located in its own territory and will therefore be beyond the reach of any court or tribunal. While the debtor state may have some assets within the jurisdiction of the courts in another country, it is frequently very difficult to levy execution against such assets, because of the law of sovereign immunity. Although most states no longer accord sovereign immunity from suit in an action in respect of a loan transaction or other debt instrument, they still enjoy a wide immunity from execution against their property. Unless the state has waived that immunity or the property is clearly in use for commercial purposes, execution or prejudgment attachment will not be available in most jurisdictions. The US Foreign Sovereign Immunities Act, section 1610(a)(2) goes further and precludes execution even against commercial property unless it has a connection with the subject matter of the action against the foreign state (a requirement which also features in a draft convention produced by the International Law Commission and currently under consideration). Embassy bank accounts in use for both commercial and governmental purposes are immune from execution in most states and the treatment of central bank accounts varies, though in the United Kingdom such accounts enjoy absolute immunity however they are used.[3] Even if immunity has been waived in respect of state property, property in the hands of separate legal entities will *prima facie* not be liable to execution in respect of obligations entered into by the state unless the forum state can be persuaded to lift the corporate veil.[4]

4   Could an analogy between international law principles on sovereign debt and national bankruptcy law be created or strengthened?

If it is thought that the prospect for orderly workout procedures for sovereign debtors would be enhanced if international law were to adopt more of the features of the institution of bankruptcy, it is necessary to examine how that might be done. The creation of a fully fledged international law of bankruptcy for sovereign states would be a massive task which is probably out of the question for the immediate future. Attention will therefore be concentrated on three features of bankruptcy law:

- The power to impose restructuring terms on creditors.

- The power to exclude the 'rogue creditor' from recourse to the courts or other unilateral action.

- The need for a tribunal which would exercise the overall supervisory and coercive role performed by national courts when exercising jurisdiction over a bankrupt corporation.

4.1　The power to impose restructuring terms on creditors

The fact that the bankruptcy laws of the United States and other countries make it possible to impose terms on a bankrupt's creditors, even where this means that they will receive substantially less than their original entitlements, is the result of a deliberate policy decision by the legislatures of those countries to afford such protection to debtors. Such national policy decisions are often recognised by other national courts and a frequently cited justification is 'comity', whereby if a court finds that there is already pending a process of universal distribution of a bankrupt's effects, it should not allow steps to be taken in its territory which would interfere with that process. The degree to which such recognition is based simply on a principle of comity is, however, doubtful.[5] In the United Kingdom, for example, the authority of a liquidator appointed under the law of the place of incorporation of a foreign corporation is recognised, Nevertheless, a US court order restraining creditors worldwide of a US corporation in Chapter 11 from issuing or prosecuting proceedings did not prevent UK creditors from freezing assets of the US corporation in the United Kingdom, particularly given the fact that release of the assets to the United States would have caused substantial prejudice to the UK creditors as the reorganization plan in question envisaged a complete withdrawal from the European market.[6] In the United States there is express statutory provision[7] for ancillary bankruptcy proceedings to be taken against assets in the United States of a debtor against whom the principal bankruptcy proceedings have been taken in another country, and comity is only one of the six criteria laid down for guidance in such cases.[8]

Returning to states, there is no international legislature capable of reducing the entitlements of sovereign debtors. A rule which permitted a majority of a state's creditors to impose their wishes on the minority or an institution like the IMF to require all creditors to accept a restructuring package could only be brought about in one of two ways.

The first possibility would be the conclusion of a treaty providing for the imposition of a restructuring package in specified circumstances. Such a treaty could be an entirely new instrument or an amendment to the constitutive treaty of one of the existing international institutions. To be effective, such a treaty would have to be accepted by all the major creditor and debtor states. In addition, those states would have to give effect to the treaty in their own national laws in such a way that private creditors would not be able to enforce debt instruments in national courts where to do so was incompatible with the terms of the restructuring package, even though they had not consented to this package. It is difficult to envisage the conclusion of such a treaty in the foreseeable future. For example, the slow progress of the International Law Commission's Draft Convention on the Jurisdictional Immunities of States and Their Property does not bode well, at least in the near future, for treaties in this area.

The second possibility is that provision for restructuring in certain specified circumstances could be incorporated in the debt instruments concluded by a particular debtor state. There is no reason in principle why a state could not include a standard clause in all its various debt instruments, when they were concluded with its different creditors, to the effect that in the event of that state being unable to meet its existing obligations within the required time, a restructuring package could be drawn up which would be binding upon each creditor, even if that creditor did not itself accept the package. There are a variety of forms such a clause might take. It could, for example, provide that if a restructuring package were agreed by a specified majority of a state's creditors, then the obligations of the state under the particular debt instrument would be amended accordingly. Alternatively, the amendment could be made conditional upon the approval of the restructuring package by the IMF or another financial institution. Provided that the same clause appeared in all of a particular state's debt instruments, then a result similar to one of the central features of national bankruptcy laws would be achieved in respect of that state. A minority creditor which opposed the restructuring package would be unable to enforce payment envisaged by the original terms of its contract because it had itself agreed in these terms to accept amendment of its entitlement if certain events should occur. In effect, each creditor would give its consent in advance to the possibility of a restructuring package, rather than having to consent to an actual package after an initial default had occurred. The sole recourse for the dissentient creditor would be to the arbitral tribunal discussed in section 4.3 below.

An essential feature of such a system would be some kind of interim protection to prevent creditors rushing to court immediately after a default to forestall the imposition of a restructuring package. Again, however, there is no reason in principle why a clause could not be included in a state's debt instruments providing that no enforcement of these instruments was possible for a certain period of time after the state defaulted on its obligations, or to provide for a period of grace after the occurrence of some specified event.

Since this system would be based on the agreement of the creditors at the time of conclusion of the debt instruments, it would have the advantage that it did not require the adoption of a new multilateral treaty. Moreover, it would provide a formal framework for the negotiations already conducted by the Paris Club and similar bodies, something which developing states have often called for. It would, however, require the inclusion of very similar provisions in all of a state's debt instruments with all its classes of creditors. This presupposes that market conditions were such that borrowers felt able to insist upon the inclusion of terms which creditors might be unlikely to welcome. It also presupposes that some formula could be found for ensuring the fairness of a rescheduling package that was sufficient to convince state, institutional and private creditors to accept the same conditions. In addition, since the basis for the system would be the consent of the parties, it would apply only to new debt. Old debt instruments would still be governed by their original terms unless the creditors concerned could be persuaded to accept modifications to them.

A further possible approach would be the establishment of bondholders' councils. This might be provided by treaty which could give such councils the exclusive right to negotiate with debtor states, though the practical difficulties of obtaining a treaty already mentioned make that a remote option. Alternatively, a model clause in debt instruments could provide for a restructuring package to be negotiated exclusively by the council on behalf of all bondholders with recourse to arbitration for dissentient bondholders. Seniority for new money would, however, probably still depend on the agreement of the bondholders at the time. Whereas bondholders are unlikely to agree in advance to a term which gives priority to new money following a restructuring (though it would theoretically be possible to envisage such a clause), it may well be that creditors would agree as part of the restructuring to grant priority for new money in return for the hope of renewed liquidity.

Gathering these threads together, from a legal point of view a blend of bondholders' councils and meetings of creditors could be envisaged, depending on whether bonds or loans were involved. In a sense, the suggestion above for a contractual mechanism to be put in place to deal with restructuring would be to provide in advance for possible solutions which might otherwise be negotiated through the Paris or London Clubs for loans and bondholders' councils for bonds. The decision on the nature of the powers to be granted by the contract to the IMF is more political than legal. The role of the IMF could, for example, be restricted to that of an expert in an advisory capacity or, depending on the view taken on its objectivity, could extend to conciliation of the parties. The proposal is, however, that whatever the contractual provisions for restructuring, dissentient creditors would retain the right to take the decision to arbitration as considered in section 4.3 below.

4.2 The power to exclude the 'rogue creditor' from recourse to the courts or other unilateral action

If the system considered in section 4.1 were adopted, the dissenting or 'rogue' creditor would have no recourse to the courts (national or international) to enforce anything other than the debt in its restructured form. The possibility has been raised, however, that even in the absence of comprehensive provision for imposing a restructuring package, the framework for achieving an orderly workout could be improved by excluding or limiting the right of a rogue creditor to have recourse to the courts. One suggestion is that this could be done by means of Article VIII(2)(b) of the IMF Articles of Agreement, which provides that:

> *Exchange contracts which involve the currency of any member and which are contrary to the exchange control regulations of that member maintained or imposed consistently with this Agreement shall be unenforceable in the territories of any member. In addition, members may by mutual accord cooperate in measures for the purposes of making the exchange control regulations of either member more effective, provided that such measures and regulations are consistent with this Agreement.*

The suggestion is that where a state suspended repayment of its debt in foreign currency in order to protect its reserves, and did so with the approval of the IMF, a debt contract which required payment to be made in a foreign currency would be contrary to that state's exchange control regulations, which had been imposed consistently with the IMF Articles of Agreement and would therefore be unenforceable in the courts of any IMF Member state. This suggestion presupposes that the term 'exchange contract' should be given a broad interpretation, applying, as one commentator said, to 'contracts which in any way affect a country's exchange resources so as to be liable to reduce them' (Mann, 1992, p. 381). The French courts would tend to support this approach, and the Cour de Cassation has declared to be sufficient *'qu'il s'agisse de contrats mettant en cause la monnaie d'un Etat membre, c'est à dire de contrats dont l'exécution affecte les ressources en devises de cet Etat, selon la définition qui en est le plus généralement donnée et qui a déjà été accuellie dans la jurisprudence'*.[9] The Article has, however, been given a much narrower interpretation by courts in the United States and in particular the United Kingdom. In the latter, the Court of Appeal in *Wilson Smithett & Cope Ltd. v Terruzzi* [1976] 1 QB 683 decided that the provision could not apply to regulations dealing with payments and transfers for merchandise transactions but could only apply to contracts for exchange of currencies, and this decision has since been approved by the House of Lords.[10] Moreover, Mann's authoritative commentary maintains that the provision is concerned with the initial legality of a contract rather than its enforceability in the light of subsequent developments (Mann, 1992, p. 370).

It seems unlikely, therefore, that any reliance can be placed upon the text as it stands. Even if it were made the subject of an interpretive declaration by the IMF supporting a broader interpretation, such an interpretation would not be binding on national courts. It would, however, be possible in principle for Article VIII(2)(b) to be amended so as to give it a role in excluding recourse to court by dissenting creditors. Although this would, again, be a controversial and difficult change to effect, the mechanism which would need to be adopted for such change is expressly provided for in Article XVIII of the Fund Agreement which permits amendments to the Agreement by a qualified majority of the members. In the majority of states, however, such a change would need to be implemented by domestic legislation. Article VIII(2)(b) would not, in any event, preclude an action by a state creditor before an international tribunal.

Another suggestion is that recourse to national courts might be barred by amending the law of sovereign immunity in a few states, such as the United Kingdom, United States, Switzerland and Germany, so as to provide that a state was immune from suit in respect of a loan transaction forming part of the state's external debt, at least where the debt had been the subject of a restructuring package approved by the IMF. The trend in these states has, however, been away from sovereign immunity for some years, and an extension of immunity would be highly controversial. Here there is an important distinction between sovereign debt and corporate debt: a change in the rules relating to bankruptcy is unlikely to have an instant effect in terms of attracting or repelling investment, whereas modification of the rules of sovereign immunity is likely to lead to overnight migration of business (through the jurisdiction clause) away from the financial centres with an unattractively broad view of sovereign immunity. Moreover, an extension of sovereign immunity to all loan transactions would go too far, while to limit it to cases in which there had been a restructuring package would confuse issues of immunity with issues of merits.

A more fruitful course might be to seek to reverse the decision in *Allied Bank* in the United States and to persuade other states that international comity required refusal to enforce a debt at the instance of a small minority of creditors who had held out against restructuring. Such a course would not, however, offer a sufficient degree of certainty since judicial reactions to arguments based on comity vary greatly between (and even within) jurisdictions. Moreover, excluding creditors from recourse to the courts in some states might serve only to bring about changes in the jurisdictional provisions of loan agreements and other instruments as creditors sought recourse to the courts in states not affected by such a change.

4.3 The need for a tribunal which would exercise the overall supervisory and coercive role performed by national courts when exercising jurisdiction over a bankrupt corporation

There is no tribunal in the existing international legal system which might play a supervisory role comparable to that of a national court in bankruptcy proceedings. The jurisdiction of the International Court of Justice is limited to cases between states and advisory opinions. In any event the court's procedures are ill suited to the exercise of a continuing supervisory role. Nor are any of the other existing tribunals suitable for such a role, even if their basic statutes were to be amended.

It would, however, be possible to create an arbitral tribunal with jurisdiction to hear cases both between states and between private creditors and a state. The Iran-United States Tribunal, for example, has heard cases brought by both state and private claimants, and the Iraq Compensation Commission has the authority to give quasi-judicial rulings in respect of both types of claims. Provision for recourse to arbitration could be built into future debt instruments, but the creation of the tribunal itself and its initial funding would probably require a treaty. Although orderly workouts are probably best achieved on the basis of negotiations between the debtor state and its creditors, the existence of an arbitral tribunal with jurisdiction over disputes between the debtor and all its various creditors could help to strengthen the framework for such negotiations. It has often been said that the main function of the US courts in bankruptcy proceedings is to supervise a framework within which a negotiated settlement between debtor and creditors can be achieved provided that that settlement is compatible with certain principles.

The creation of such an arbitral tribunal would both strengthen the negotiating process and produce the dual benefit of avoiding recourse to national courts. At the same time it would provide a means of recourse for dissentient creditors thereby warding off charges, whether under the European Convention or otherwise, that creditors are being deprived of a hearing. In order for it to be effective, the arbitral tribunal would have to be seized of disputes on which it is being asked to adjudicate so that national courts would stay court proceedings on the grounds of the arbitration clause. The process envisaged would be in two stages with the IMF/bondholders' councils/majority of creditors sanctioning restructuring under the contract, combined with a right of recourse to a single unified arbitral tribunal, on the grounds, for example, that the rescheduling goes beyond what is permitted by the contract.

5   Conclusion

Although some aspects of the international treatment of state debt default resemble aspects of national bankruptcy laws – for example, the collective approach and acceptance of restructuring plans by the Paris Club – international law does not at present provide a legal framework consciously designed to encourage this process. The creation of such a framework presents very great difficulties. The important point to bear in mind is that what is needed most is a way to indicate official, international approval for a debtor's course of action. It would, however, be possible to adopt some features of the Paris Club through the incorporation into state debt instruments of certain model clauses, the scope of which will depend on the degree of consensus that can be reached between lenders and states and also on what is regarded as necessary in the interests of efficiency. A model clause might cover such issues as:

- Obligations of state amended if restructuring package agreed by specified majority of creditors.

- Obligations of state amended if restructuring package approved by IMF or other institution.

- Obligations of state amended if restructuring package agreed by bondholders' council exercising exclusive right to negotiate with the state.

- Clause which permits restructuring package expressly permits package to grant seniority to new money.

- In the event of default by debtor state, no action to be taken by creditors for a specified period.

- In the event of default by debtor state, compulsory reference to a dedicated arbitral tribunal for multipartite arbitration of all claims arising out of the loan or bond.

- Failure of debtor state to incorporate similar provision in future loan agreements constitutes an act of default.

Unlike bankruptcy law, however, this approach is based upon the consent of the creditors and debtor states, rather than the imposition by central authority of an interference with the normal functioning of contracts.

Notes

1. If agreement is reached on a rescheduling package, the negotiations would tend to culminate in the creditors entering into a final agreement with the borrower and an interbank agreement among themselves (MacLean, 1989, p. 79).

2. For a summary of the issues in this case, see the Appendix to this paper.

3. S. 14(4) State Immunity Act 1978.

4. See, for example, *Letelier v Republic of Chile* 748 F.2d 790 (2d Cir. 1984) where an attempt to execute judgment against Chile by attacking property of its national airline was rejected *inter alia* for this reason.

5. Dicey and Morris (1993), p. 1138.

6. *Felixstowe Dock and Railway Co. v US Line Inc.* (1989) QB 360.

7. Section 304, United States Bankruptcy Code.

8. The other factors are:

(i) the just treatment of all holders of claims against or interests in such estate;

(ii) protection of claim holders in the United States against prejudice and inconvenience in the processing of claims in such foreign proceedings;

(iii) prevention of preferential or fraudulent dispositions of property of such estate;

(iv) distribution of proceeds of such estate substantially in accordance with the order prescribed by this title;

(v) if appropriate, the provision of an opportunity for a fresh start for the individual that such foreign proceeding concerns.

9. ' ... that it be a question of contracts concerning the money of a member state, i.e. of contracts whose execution affects the foreign exchange reserves of this state, according to the definition which is most commonly given and which has already been accepted in jurisprudence.'

10. *United City Merchants (Investments) Ltd. v Royal Bank of Canada* (1983) 1 AC 168.

Appendix

The *Allied Bank* litigation

Allied Bank International v. Banco Credito Agricola de Cartago 757 F2d 516 (1985) 88 ILR 62; US Court of Appeals (2nd Circuit)

Allied was the agent for a syndicate of 39 banks which held promissory notes issued by three state-owned Costa Rican banks. The notes were payable in US dollars in New York. The obligations to pay were registered with the Central Bank, which suspended all external debt payments. Allied sued the Costa Rican banks. At the first instance, the District Court (566 F Supp 1440; SDNY 1983) held that the actions were barred by the act of state doctrine because Griesa J held that the decision of a US court on the debt policy of the Costa Rican government could embarrass the US government in its relations with Costa Rica. The syndicate then concluded an agreement on refinancing, but one of the syndicate banks (Fidelity Union Trust of New Jersey) did not accept the agreement, and Allied appealed to the Court of Appeals on its behalf.

In its first decision, the Court of Appeals upheld the District Court's decision, holding that the restructuring agreement was in line with US policy because the US government supported the economic strategy of Costa Rica. On an application for rehearing, however, the US Department of Justice submitted an *amicus curiae* brief to the effect that the United States supported the conclusion of negotiated restructuring under the auspices of the IMF, the central feature of which was that although the parties were encouraged to renegotiate conditions of payment, in the absence of agreement by the creditor, the obligations of the debtor to the creditor remained valid. The Department argued that Costa Rica's attempted unilateral restructuring of private obligations was inconsistent with this system of international cooperation and negotiation and thus contrary to US policy. The Department also maintained that its position on the sanctity of private international debt, in the absence of agreement from the specific creditor, was consistent with its support for and aid to Costa Rica and other Latin American states.

The Court of Appeals then vacated its earlier decision and handed down a new decision in favour of Allied. The Court held that the debts were located in the United States and that the Costa Rican action was an attempt to take property located outside its territory (the property being the right to receive payment in New York). The Court said:

> *The Costa Rican government's unilateral attempt to repudiate private, commercial obligations is inconsistent with the orderly resolution of international debt problems. It is similarly contrary to the interests of the US, a major source of private international credit* (p. 522).

It is understood that the case was subsequently settled with the US government encouraging Fidelity Union to accept the package agreed by the rest of the syndicate.

References

Delaume, G. (1994), 'The Foreign Sovereign Immunities Act and Public Debt Litigation: Some Fifteen Years Later', *American Journal of International Law* 88, p. 257.

Dicey and Morris (1993), *The Conflict of Laws*, 12th edn., Sweet and Maxwell.

Gold, J. (1979), *Legal and Institutional Aspects of the International Monetary System*, IMF Publications.

Hess, B. (1993), 'The International Law Commission's Draft Convention on the Jurisdictional Immunities of States and their Property', *European Journal of International Law* 4, p. 269.

MacLean, R.G. (1989), 'Legal Aspects of the External Debt', *Recueil des Cours* 214, p. 35.

Mann, F.A. (1992), *The Legal Aspect of Money,* Oxford, Oxford University Press.

Rendell, R.S. (ed.) (1983), *International Financial Law*, Euromoney Publications.

Annex 4

Multilateral sovereign debt restructuring: The Paris Club and the London Club

Giovanni Vitale
Birkbeck College, London

1   The Paris Club

The Paris Club is the forum where credits issued, guaranteed or insured by creditor governments are rescheduled or refinanced. It is not an institution but a set of rules and procedures, and its membership is determined case by case: in general it includes some or all of the 15 biggest OECD countries and always the G–7 countries.

Over time the Paris Club has extended its procedures beyond mere rescheduling sessions. It engages in two other sorts of activities: methodology sessions and *tours d'horizon*. The first activity involves discussions about debt strategy innovations, rescheduling formulas used by the Club, the Club's operating procedures or particularly complex country cases. The second, occupying one day a month, is dedicated to the discussion of countries which are likely to apply to the Club in the near future, or those which the Club wants to monitor closely, or any other case one of the creditors wants to discuss. Representatives of the IMF and the World Bank are invited to present the state of their relations with the interested debtor country. The principal aim of the Paris Club, however, is to reschedule the debtor's debt.

1.1   Rescheduling sessions

The negotiation between the debtor and the Paris Club does not begin automatically. Countries might be advised not to apply for a debt rescheduling to preserve the goodwill of the markets, and to implement import substituting and expenditure reducing policies instead. Some creditors, perhaps because of a close link with the debtor, might agree to refinance its debt, that is to provide the money to maintain its solvency (for example, France to African ex-colonies and the United States to Latin America). The debtor applies for a rescheduling with the Paris Club following the advice of the creditor countries, once the *imminent default* (i.e. insolvency) has been documented. To ascertain this the Paris Club rearranges the income and expenditure components of the IMF projection of the balance of payments of the debtor country for the coming year[1]: if expenditure exceeds income, a situation of imminent default exists. In this way the creditor countries reduce the risk of 'moral hazard' (that is, the debtor using disposable foreign exchange for uses other than debt payment) and maintain the principle that rescheduling is an exceptional solution to the debtor country's problem. On the other hand, the debtor can avoid restrictive policies like cutting imports, devaluation or diverting local products to export markets. The Paris Club has never rescheduled a debt without the practical application of this principle.[2]

Following the application, the date of the meeting can be arranged immediately if an agreement with the IMF over a readjustment programme has already been made. Otherwise the debtor is reminded of this precondition, which is known as *appropriate conditionality*. This requirement reflects the willingness of creditors to maintain the rescheduling operations as extraordinary: the operation is only justified in a much wider policy context, oriented to re-establish the solvency of the debtor.

This requirement was not formalized until 1966, after the Argentine experience of continuous rescheduling owing to the lack of any structural adjustment programme. A stand-by agreement is not a strict requirement of the Paris Club, but it can reschedule if the debtor country also has a Structural Adjustment Facility agreement with the IMF (as in the case of low income countries).

The procedure introduces a complication. If the IMF has to agree a stand-by arrangement, it wants to know what kind of debt relief the creditors will accept in order to be sure that the IMF loan will be repaid. The creditors, of course, want to see the stand-by agreement before the rescheduling, for exactly the same reason. This problem has been solved differently in the rescheduling of different countries[3], but always with a measure of coordination among debtor, creditors and IMF.

The precondition of appropriate conditionality has led to the exclusion of the Paris Club procedures in the negotiation of debt rescheduling of non-IMF member countries.[4]

Once the date of the Paris Club meeting has been arranged, both the creditors and the debtor, depending on their different national procedures, have to prepare the introductory document. Each creditor country presents its view of the debtor's situation and proposes possible measures by defining the margins of flexibility it is willing to accept on each of the debts which are going to be negotiated, remembering that the negotiation has to take place with the other creditors too. The debtor, on the other hand, has to ask for the creditors' help and therefore has to prepare a document detailing the analysis and the strategies for recovering from the external imbalance problem.[5]

At the meeting the chairman invites the debtor country to present its request, and a round-table discussion follows with submissions from representatives of the international organisations (IMF, World Bank, the regional bank of development concerned and UNCTAD) and the creditors, in alphabetical order (Germany is often first, which means that it has greater power to dictate the line of the discussion than the other creditors). The creditors then meet without the debtor and agree a first proposal to present to the debtor. The chairperson meets the debtor privately and makes the creditors' proposal. Generally the debtor does not accept the first proposal and makes a counter-offer for the chairperson to take back to the creditors. The process goes on until all parties agree; this could also involve consultation between the delegations and their own governments.

The process described above is based on the principle of *Agreement by Consensus*, which means that the creditors must approve each decision they take in the negotiating progress unanimously. Agreement is usually reached relatively quickly and is formalized in an Agreed Minute which is signed by the parties. The final agreement has to conform to the principle of *Equitable Burden Sharing*. This means that creditors participating in the Paris Club have to share the burden fairly: the objective of the Paris Club in the debt relief operation is to 'save' the credits, and the costs of this must be spread among the interested parties in proportion to the future benefit. In practice, this issue has been solved by linking the creditors' participation in the debt relief operation to their financial exposure in the debtor country. Without this principle, a single creditor might try to seek a bilateral agreement with the debtor to reduce its part of the burden of the operation, thus leaving a larger amount of debt to be rescheduled among the others.[6]

In order to achieve this result all the credits extended before a certain date, regardless of their terms and purpose, are rescheduled with the same grace and repayment periods. The interest rate is allowed to vary from creditor to creditor to take account of their different institutional environments. The practical application of the principle of equitable burden sharing has been controversial every time the debt relief package includes new lines of credit to the debtor. In particular, officially guaranteed new export credit has been very controversial, because the 'bridge financing' and long-term development funding are provided by the G–10 (closely linked to the IMF) and by the World Bank respectively.

The creditors participating in the Paris Club further protect themselves from possible 'free-riders' by inserting a 'non-discriminatory' clause in the Agreed Minute. This commits the debtor not to accept worse conditions from these creditors than those granted by the participating official creditors. If the Agreed Minute is not respected, the participating creditors have to be paid more rapidly. This is a disincentive for the free riding of both debtor and creditor. The debtor cannot seek extra debt relief outside of the Paris Club on worse conditions, and the creditor has the incentive to participate in the Paris Club, because its attempt to free ride could lead to the default of the debtor. Concessional bilateral reschedulings are allowed, and they do not affect the Paris Club agreement.

Finally, the Paris Club rescheduling agreement also invites the debtor to seek debt relief from its private creditors, i.e. commercial banks[7], on *comparable terms*. The issue of 'bailing out the banks' as the possible consequence of the exclusion of private banks from the debt relief operation was raised in the 1970s, when the exposure of commercial banks first became relevant. In that case, it would have been unfair for the official creditors, using public money, to grant debt relief to debtors which would have been used to repay the debt to the private banks. This is why the concept of 'comparable treatment' arose in the Paris Club negotiations. The country must seek a measure of debt relief from banks which is as generous in the context of normal commercial lending as is the official relief granted by the Paris Club in the context of the official lending. The application of this principle has been quite different. For instance, in the case of Zaire (1976–9), the official creditors conditioned their debt relief negiotations on their approval of similar operations between the debtor and its private creditors. In some cases the Paris Club and the banks applied more or less the same terms of debt relief, and in others (Poland, Liberia, Togo 1978–84) the comparable treatment was very hard to achieve.

The 'multilateral lending' institutions (IMF, the World Bank, Asian, African and Inter-American development banks and other institutions like the European Investment Bank and a special OPEC fund) are exempt from the sharing of rescheduling. There two reasons for this. First, they have both the creditor and the debtor as their members, so both benefit from the exemption, although the shadow cost of sharing is higher for the creditors than it is for the debtors, because in general debtor countries have a lower level of participation in multilateral institutions than creditor countries. Second, these institutions are supposed to contribute to the burden sharing by providing new loans to the debtor. This has not always happened, especially in the case of minor institutions.

The signing of the Agreed Minute does not conclude the renegotiation process. The rescheduling agreement comes into effect only after bilateral agreements have been reached between the debtor and each of the creditors. These agreements must be concluded six to eight months after the signing of the Agreed Minute. The incentive to do so is that all the debt related to bilateral agreements not signed in the prescribed terms is considered in arrears, and this can preclude IMF disbursement of the money for the stabilization programme. In addition, no further rescheduling is possible if the debtor has not previously signed the bilateral agreement referring to past rescheduling agreements. The bilateral agreement is very important because it is here that the 'moratorium' interest rate[8] has to be defined. This is because different countries have different regulatory constraints, and it is impossible to define a unique interest rate in the Paris Club meeting.

1.2   Rescheduling terms

The general objective of the Paris Club is not to reschedule the whole stock of debt, but only the payments on existing stock falling due in a particular period of time, called the 'consolidation period'. Even these payments are not wholly rescheduled and the conditions of the rescheduling vary from case to case, evolving over time and reflecting the bargaining power the debtor country had in relation to its solvency condition. The variables on which the creditors and debtor have to agree are described below.

1.2.1   The cut-off date
This is the latest date by which the debt contract must be signed in order for the payments arising from that debt to be considered eligible for rescheduling. The idea is to avoid the uncertainty that would lead the creditors (especially export credit agencies) to refuse to give any new credit to the debtor if it could be rescheduled in the Paris Club. This could work against the interests of the Paris Club negotiators, since the cut-off of new inflows of capital could worsen the solvency position of the debtor. In general the cut-off date is set at about six to nine months before the scheduled Paris Club meeting.

1.2.2   The consolidation period
This is the period of time in which the payments to be rescheduled fall due. In general it overlaps the IMF programme coverage. The reason for this is that although aimed to rebuild the debtor's solvency, the debt rescheduling agreement must not modify the nature of the original debt relationship.

1.2.3   Categories of debt considered
Two categories of debt are always excluded: short-term credit (up to one year) and post-cut-off debt. Immediately after comes the previously rescheduled debt, although in some cases the Paris Club has not been able to exclude this debt from the negotiations.[9] Thus the maturities falling due in the consolidation period of the medium- to long-term credits contracted before the cut-off date are the object of rescheduling.[10]

1.2.4   The 'classical' terms of rescheduling
In general, the payments are rescheduled on the following terms: five years of grace; semi-annual payments of the principal in years six to ten; moratorium interest rate (defined in the bilateral agreement) designed to keep intact the net present value of the debt (no grant component). The Paris Club has recently introduced the possibility of repaying on 'blended terms', which allow the repayment of the principal to be spread over a longer

time period (up to 15 years) but with a shorter grace period. Repayments of the principal rise gradually over time. These are the 'standard' rescheduling terms applied by the Paris Club, but it is worth pointing out that these terms have not always been applied unequivocally in the history of Paris Club renegotiations. Indonesia, India and Kampuchea, for instance, rescheduled the whole stock of their debt in the period from 1966–74, with a 30-year amortization period. This happened many years before 1988, when the Paris Club formally agreed to consider conceding some 'grant component' in the debt relief process with a very indebted and poor debtor.

1.3   The terms for the poorest countries

In the late 1980s the problem of the sovereign debt of the poorest countries exploded, leading the Paris Club to revise its operations. From 1988 to 1990 three new possible terms of rescheduling poor and very poor countries' debt were approved. They contained a grant element, that is they accepted a partial reduction of the net present value of the debt. The reasons for this were very simple. First, insisting on applying the 'classical terms' to these countries simply did not make sense any more in particularly disastrous situations. Second, not surprisingly most of the debt of these countries was official, with the banks having very little exposure, which avoided the possible 'bail out the banks' argument and allowed the creditors more scope to restore the debtor's financial situation.

1.3.1   'Lower-middle income countries': The Houston terms

At the Houston Summit in 1990, it was agreed that the Paris Club would apply new rescheduling terms to debtor countries qualifying as 'low-middle income countries'. To be eligible a country has to meet the following criteria:

*   GNP per head must be below $1,195 (in 1990 US dollars).

*   The Paris Club debt has to be at least 150% of the private debt.

*   The country must have a particularly negative standing in a test of indebtedness based on debt/GNP, debt/exports and scheduled debt service/exports ratios.

In this case the debtor country can choose to repay the export credit agency rescheduled debt over 15 years with eight years of grace, and official development assistance debt over 20 years with ten years of grace.

1.3.2   'Very low-income countries': The Toronto and Trinidad terms

The Toronto terms defined by the Paris Club at the 1988 Toronto meeting were the first to contain a grant element. They have now been replaced in practice by the Trinidad terms. To be eligible for rescheduling under Toronto terms, the country had to be very poor (GNP per head below $610) and very indebted (debt service/export ratio not below 25%). In addition, the country had to be listed among the World Bank's 'International Development Association' (IDA) countries. For instance, Nigeria, although substantially meeting the criteria, could not reschedule under these terms because it was not among the IDA countries.

The *Toronto terms* consist of a 'menu' of three different options:

(A)   One-third write-off of the rescheduled debt, and the remainder rescheduled at commercial rate of interest over 14 years; seven or eight years of grace.

(B)   100% of the maturities to be rescheduled at a commercial rate over 25 years; 14 years of grace.

(C)   The interest rate reduced by 3.5 percentage points or halved (whichever the smaller) and 14 years of repayment; seven or eight years of grace.

Options A and C have a grant component which reduces the discounted value of the rescheduled debt. In fact these two options represent a transfer of resources from the creditors to the debtor. For this reason the creditor countries agree that the grant component of these terms should not to be financed out of the aid programme to the debtor country. In addition these terms apply (applied) only to commercial credits, because the creditors wanted the aid credits to be repaid at their whole present value, although they accepted the possibility of stretching out the repayment period for these creditors: 25 years with 14 years of grace. Finally, the application of these terms is at the complete discretion of the creditors, who choose the debtor country concerned, the option to apply and the category of debt rescheduled.

The *Trinidad terms,* effective since December 1991, were introduced to alleviate further the burden of debt on the same countries that were eligible for the Toronto terms. The Trinidad terms also consist of a menu of options whose application is subject to the same rules as the Toronto terms:

(D)   50% reduction of the maturities consolidated and repayment over 23 years; six years of grace.

(E)   100% of the maturities rescheduled at a reduced interest rate to produce a reduction of 50% in the net present value of the debt; repayment over 23 years and no grace period.

(F)   100% maturities rescheduled at a commercial rate over 25 years; 16 years of grace.

In general no further concessional rescheduling (a re-rescheduling is possible, but under the 'classical' terms) is allowed by the Paris Club on the maturities already rescheduled at concessional terms, but if the debtor follows a long (3–4 years) period of readjustment under the supervision of the IMF, the Paris Club can consider giving relief to up to 50% of the whole stock of debt.

2   The London Club

The London Club is the forum in which the credits extended by commercial banks (without a creditor government guarantee) are rescheduled. Like the Paris Club, the London Club is a set of conventional rules, and its membership is defined case by case, depending on the private banks involved in the negotiations. Unlike the Paris Club, however, the name of the forum is not related to any fixed venue or continuing secretariat: London Club sessions can be held in places other than London. The first London Club session was held to reschedule the debt of Zaire in 1976, but it was during the debt crisis of the early 1980s that it became an important player in debt restructuring operations.

2.1   Procedures

Once the restructuring process starts, the banks involved in lending in the debtor country form the 'steering committee' or 'advisory group'. The steering committee generally comprises up to 15 banks, designated by the debtor country, and acts on behalf of and as a liaison group with all bank creditors. Typically, membership of the committee is determined by the banks' financial exposure in the debtor country and by regional considerations. The bank with the highest exposure chairs the committee; the others act as regional coordinators.

The first action of the steering committee is to appoint an 'economic subcommittee' to make a forecast of the debtor's financing gap. This is used in negotiations with both the debtor and with the IMF. The banks rely on the ability of the IMF to monitor the policy conduct of the debtor (banks showed in the cases of Peru (1978) and Poland (1980) that they have very little leverage of their own to enforce compliance with specific economic policy targets in debtor countries). Thus they tend to link their restructuring plans to some form of IMF 'seal of approval', in particular when these plans involve the provision of 'new money'. This means that private banks, official creditors and the IMF are all engaged in a negotiation about the share of debt relief each of them has to grant to the debtor. The important point to note is that because of the nature of the original loan contracted between the banks and the creditors, there is little incentive for the banks to seek unilateral restructuring, or to free ride by leaving the costs of restructuring to other creditors. In the 'syndicated loans' from each bank to a single debtor country four clauses appear which demonstrate the cohesiveness and strength of the lenders during the restructuring process:

- *The sharing clause*. This seeks to ensure that no creditor can be discriminated against when a debtor makes payments (all banks share, in proportion to their share of total lending to a country, in any payments made to banks by that country).

- *The pari passu and negative pledge clauses*. These seek to ensure equality of treatment of the loans under any specific loan agreement with all other loans to the same borrower, by giving equal right of payment and equal right of collateral, thus ensuring that no creditor can receive a prior right to security in preference to any other.

- *The mandatory prepayment clause*. This ensures the equal treatment of all creditors should there be a repayment prior to the maturity of the loan.

In addition, to avoid the problem of free riding by non-participating banks, the London Club inserts in the final agreement a non-discriminatory clause, whereby the debtor country undertakes not to give more favourable treatment to any other creditor than that agreed with the London Club.

The negotiation process can be claimed to be less efficient than the Paris Club's because of the different relationship between the 'negotiator' and the creditors represented. Whereas in the Paris Club the 'negotiators' and the creditors are one and the same, in the London Club they are not. If the banks on the advisory committee do not consult the other banks at each stage of the negotiations, they do take care to keep them informed, and in some cases a series of presentations are made to local banks at various centres around the world. Considering the large number of banks that are often involved, this process can be very time consuming, and the London Club's rule that the final agreement has to be approved by 90–95% of the creditors has not really reduced the time involved. In addition, the case-by-case approach used by the creditors in the restructuring negotiations carries with it some additional time-consuming tasks: consideration and reconciliation of the debt data from either side; establishing criteria for exclusion or inclusion; co-financing with multilateral organisations (i.e. the World Bank). These tasks are delegated to subcommittees.

2.2   Restructuring terms

The main difference between official and private restructuring operations is in the eligible credits: banks never reschedule maturities falling due as interest payments. On the other hand, banks try to have a more global approach to the problem, restructuring the whole stock of debt. In general, the interest payments are met by 'new money' so that the banks can maintain both lending operations as 'performing loans' in their books.[11] As in the Paris Club negotiations and for the same reasons, a cut-off date is established in agreement with the debtor. The first category of credits restructured is medium-term uncollateralized ones, but apart from the interest arrears there is no *a priori* exemption of any categories of debt from the restructuring process.

2.3   Restructuring process

The difference between private and sovereign lending is reflected in the different approach to the restructuring process. The private banks always try not to jeopardize the future recourse of the debtor country to the capital market. That is why although they never restructure interest payments, they have negotiated other forms of debt relief during the restructuring operations and have also opened new lines of credit in connection with the debtor's fulfilment of its obligations with the IMF.

Commercial bank restructuring processes are conducted on a case-by-case basis. In general, interest charged on the restructured debt has always been at a penalty rate, calculated as a premium over the Libor rate. In addition, spreads have been always higher and maturities shorter for a debtor's first restructuring, and the consolidation period has never been more than one year. All the operations are coordinated with the IMF in order to balance the adjustment needs and the financing for the coming year. Banks have never been committed to medium-term restructuring. They prefer to agree to subsequent restructuring if the adjustment programme has been implemented successfully. In subsequent restructurings the debtor has always enjoyed lower spreads and longer repayment and grace periods. Also important are the MYRA (Multi-Year Restructuring Agreements), which in addition to these rewards for the 'well-behaved' debtor include an extension of the consolidation period, as in the Paris Club negotiations. Similar to the Paris Club's MYRA, these multi-year agreements oblige the debtor country to disclose its economic data to the creditor banks, so they can check the degree of implementation of the readjustment plan agreed with the IMF and compare it with the individual credit policy each bank pursues.

When the readjustment policies are not followed, or no improvement of economic performance is evident, the banks have tended to take a more conservative position, stretching out the terms of repayment of the existing debt but reducing the provision of new money, and practically closing the capital market to the 'bad' debtor.

In a London Club negotiation it is also possible for a creditor to 'escape', that is to withdraw its exposure in the debtor country by selling back its share of credit at a discounted price. This is in the interest of everyone: of the debtor, which enjoys an indirect form of debt relief;[12] of the escaping bank, which given its corporate strategies takes the optimal action;[13] and of the remaining banks, which see the expected present value of the repayment of their share of debt increased.[14]

2.5   The London Club: An historical perspective

The London Club's working procedure outlined above has to be considered as the outcome of the changing practice of private banks' debt restructuring. This process is marked by different stages consolidated after 1987.

Before the world debt crisis of the 1980s the few restructuring operations private banks were involved in consisted of the rescheduling of principal payments in arrears, without any provision of new money. The rationale behind this approach was that the debt restructuring had to provide temporary relief for debtors suffering from balance-of-payments problems. The 1980s debt crisis caused the banks' debt restructuring to develop into a more standardized and efficient process because of the increased number of cases, the possibility to accumulate information on debtor country statistics, the establishment of precedents to deal with serial rescheduling, and the existence of the steering committees.

The categories of debt considered for restructuring were principal payments and the arrears on them falling due approximately 12 months after the onset of the negotiations. In some cases the consolidation period was extended to two years and occasionally three. In a few exceptional cases interest arrears were also rescheduled, but none of the agreements considered the restructuring of future interest payments. The effect of these agreements was to restructure in all but two cases at least 80% of the principal payments falling due in the consolidation period; and in over half the whole amount was restructured.

The banks' basic approach in the restructuring process was not to reschedule payments at less than market-related interest rates. This, coupled with the exceptional magnitude of most of the debt to be restructured, characterizes the evolution of the banks' debt restructuring.

In the first phase (1983–4), the terms and conditions applied in the renegotiation process could be generally classified as emergency operations (one to two years) heavily penalizing the debtor for falling behind in its debt obligations. Eleven reprogramming agreements in this period provided for maturities of seven to eight years, carrying a spread over Libor of not less than 2% plus an average commission of 1.10% on the amount of debt restructured. Ecuador, Mexico, Yugoslavia and the Southern Cone countries restructured most of their debt.

Latin American countries made the most concessions to the banks in terms of transferring private-sector debt to the public sector and clearing up arrears. Mexico restructured the largest amount of debt in this period and also bore the largest restructuring costs (as it did over the whole period). Other countries such as Brazil, Nigeria and Peru made fewer concessions, but restructured a significantly smaller amount of debt.

The duration of the negotiations varied from three months to six months for two main reasons: on the debtor side, there was little resistance to accepting or implementing IMF agreements; on the creditor side, even the smaller banks seemed to be willing to accept proportional increases in their exposure. This first phase was characterized by the punitive terms imposed on the debtors.

The second phase in 1985–6 produced both more resources and much softer terms. Fifteen agreements were signed in this period, and the amount rescheduled rose by almost 300%, but new money and other facilities were sharply curtailed. The average consolidation period more than doubled, the average spread over Libor was reduced to 1.18%, maturities stretched to almost 13 years and commissions disappeared. On the other hand, the period between the agreement in principle and the formal signing of the final agreement tended to increase appreciably, as difficulties with meeting the IMF programme targets and the reluctance of smaller banks to continue extending their exposure came into play. Nevertheless, in this period debtors (especially Mexico) enjoyed much improved treatment.

In the third phase of the private debt restructuring (starting in 1987), banks maintained the existing levels of exposure but provided only two countries with new money: Argentina and Mexico. Other facilities declined sharply in this period. Only six agreements were signed because fewer debtors could maintain the pace of policy restructuring imposed by the IMF adjustment programmes. Several could not even maintain their interest repayments, let alone capital repayments on the original or the already restructured debt. At the same time there was a marked improvement in the restructuring conditions.

Average consolidation periods increased again (up to 63 months), the spreads over Libor fell to less than 1% and maturities lengthened to 18 years. Some countries such as Argentina, Mexico, the Philippines and Venezuela restructured large proportions of their debt (82–97%), while Chile restructured only 37%.

The Mexican agreement was the first real renegotiation agreement, in the sense that it was the first agreement presenting a comprehensive approach. It encompassed the restructuring of previous agreements over a long-term horizon and incorporated contingency clauses with respect to growth and export prices. The lengthening of the period required for the formal agreement to be concluded made evident the difficulty of reconciling the smaller US and European banks' strategies with these agreements. It can be argued, however, that this third phase held the promise of a significant improvement in the debtor countries' treatment.

The last important feature of the 1980s restructuring is the provision of bridging finance during the debt renegotiation period, pending agreement on new medium-term finance. This kind of financing was provided by commercial banks, governments and the Bank of International Settlements (BIS), which played an important role in providing bridging finance to non-BIS members too.

In the context of the proposal of a new bankruptcy procedure, the impossibility of conducting a single debt restructuring negotiation for both official and private debt clearly arises from the different legal nature of the two obligations. In the first case, the governments of the creditor countries act as administrators of someone else's money (the creditor country's taxpayers). They cannot therefore take 'risky' decisions linked to the restructuring of the stock of the debt, like refinancing, without political support. Banks, on the other hand, are private firms so that they only have to respect their managers' decisions and the shareholders' interests. This does not mean, however, that is impossible to design some coordination mechanism able to reduce the inefficiencies arising from the existence of different categories of creditors: governments, private banks and the multilateral institutions.

Notes

1. This assures the objectivity of the assessment of the balance-of-payments status of a debtor country. In addition, as Dooley (1995) points out, the IMF assessment is valued by the creditor for its ability to incorporate 'private' information that the debtor government would never supply to the creditor country directly.

2. In the case of the Pakistan rescheduling in 1980, the operations were led outside the Paris Club context, to avoid creating a precedent. In the case of the 'two-years' rescheduling of Peruvian debt in 1979–80, the principle was saved by making the continuation of the rescheduling plan in the second year conditional on a second IMF evaluation of a new financing gap for that year (and on a new stand-by agreement with the IMF itself).

3. In the case of Brazil (1983), because of the large amount of debt owing to the banks, the rescheduling conditions were discussed inside the IMF as a part of a whole package including the stand-by agreement. In the case of Sudan (1982), because of the scarcity of private credit, the IMF arranged a stand-by which the Executive Board approved provisionally, that is the agreement did not go into effect until adequate debt relief with the Paris Club had been agreed.

4. Poland (1981), Cuba (1982), Mozambique (1984). These cases were very problematic in different respects. First, the normal economic indicators were very difficult to interpret, and this prejudiced the ability of the creditors' economic task force to evaluate the state of insolvency and the policy programme to suggest to the debtor. Second, it was impossible to control the debtors' behaviour. Poland, for instance, paid back all its private debt, leaving little foreign exchange for the official creditors.

5. This is one of the main points of concern for the debtor countries. Countries applying for the first time incur very high costs for their application and presentation because they have to consult 'experts' in the preparation of the documents.

6. The incentive for the debtor is the possibility of saving on the price of rescheduling (i.e. getting better terms of repayment of the consolidated debt).

7. Suppliers, i.e. exporters of the creditor countries, are not considered. If they have private credit lines with insolvent importers and their credits are not guaranteed by an official agency, their credits are not considered.

8. This is the interest rate charged on the amount of debt rescheduled.

9. In addition, on the request of the debtor country, the Paris Club has agreed to reduce the private-sector debt to be rescheduled by half when it is not a large component of the rescheduling. This was intended to avoid the loss of the confidence of the export credit agencies in the ability of the private debtors to repay their debt, which could have undermined the possibility of opening new lines of credit for the same debtors.

10. In addition, the payments falling due in the consolidation period to a particular debtor country which are below a certain level (defined by the size of the debtor's obligations and its capacity to pay) are excluded from the rescheduling. In this case the creditor interested is said to be *de minimis*.

11. And the debtor country is not excluded from the international markets. This consideration is very important. It can be considered an actual rule of the game; for example, the recent Bulgarian debt restructuring, because it involved some interest payments, took the country out of the market for new lending (Houben, 1995).

12. To close its exposure in a country, the bank has to demand the repayment of the loan, but on conditions set up in the context of the restructuring process. This cannot be done therefore without considering the need to preserve the other (not exiting) banks' interests. The convenience for the debtor of these buybacks depends upon the debtor's access to foreign reserves: the lower the level of foreign reserves available to the debtor, the higher will be the opportunity cost of diverting these reserves from productive uses to debt service.

13. Williamson (1988) discusses the incentives some banks might have to sell their loans at distress prices. The first is a pessimistic view of the future debt servicing ability of the debtor country, which interacts with the discount rate the banks use to weight the future; the second might be the high cost of administration a loan carries, coupled with a relatively small exposure in the debtor country. In addition, banks might have other relationships with the debtor country apart from the single loan (for example, with banks in the debtor country). The price at which some banks might be willing to sell the debtor's obligation might also be low because of the tax system in the creditor's country, which could create some incentive to act in this way. The interesting question here is why the 'optimistic' banks do not buy the 'pessimistic' loans. There might be two answers: either the optimists consider themselves already optimally exposed with respect to that particular country, or the fear of the debtor's reduced willingness to service debt originated from sources other than the original relationship.

14. As the Debt Relief Laffer Curve argument illustrates.

References

Brau, E. and Williams, R. (1983), 'Recent Multilateral Debt Restructurings with Official and Bank Creditors', International Monetary Fund Occasional Paper No. 25.

Dillon, K.B. (1985), *Recent Developments in External Debt Restructuring*, Washington D.C., International Monetary Fund.

Dooley, P.M. (1995), 'The IMF and the 1982 and 1994 Crises: Who is in Charge?', paper presented at the CEPR workshop 'Political Economy, Sovereign Debt and the IMF', Cambridge, 7/8 July.

Hooley, H.A. (1987), 'Developing Country Debt: The Role of the Commercial Banks', Chatham House Paper No. 35.

Knox, D. (1990), *Latin American Debt. Facing Facts*, Oxford International Institute.

Rieffel, A. (1994), 'The Paris Club 1979–93', *Columbia Journal of Transnational Law* 23, pp. 83–110.

Sevigny, D. (1990), *The Paris Club. An Inside View*, North-South Institute, Ottawa.

United Nations Centre on Transnational Corporations (1991), 'Transnational Banks and the International Debt Crisis', prepared by a team headed by M. Mortimore, United Nations, New York.

Williamson, J. (1988), 'Voluntary Approaches to Debt Relief', *Policy Analyses in International Economics*, Institute for International Economics, Washington D.C..